The Happiness Manual

21 Ways to stay *Happy*
no matter what

The Happiness Manual

21 Ways to stay *Happy* no matter what

ARUNA JOSHI

EMBASSY BOOKS
www.embassybooks.in

THE HAPPINESS MANUAL ©Aruna Joshi 2018

First Edition 2018

Published in India by:
Embassy Book Distributors
120, Great Western Building,
Maharashtra Chamber of Commerce Lane,
Fort, Mumbai 400 023, India
Tel: (+9122) -30967415, 22819546
Email: info@embassybooks.in
www.embassybooks.in

ISBN: 978-93-86451-04-0

Cover Design by Sonal Churi

Layout and typesetting by Sonal Churi & Gangaram Dhuri

Printed & Bound in India by Repro India Ltd., Navi Mumbai

FOREWORD

Happiness as a topic is like relationships and politics – everyone has an opinion about it, and ironically, most of the views held by people are based on the views of others. 'I think I will be happy when I am rich' – an opinion given to me by those desiring to be rich. When confronted with a question, 'What do you want from life?' or 'What is your long-term goal?' A very common reply is, "All I want is to be happy." A splendid decision by all means. What gets most respondents flustered is when asked, "So what makes you happy?" This is where the expressions start changing into thoughtful ones.

So at first, we think of a bunch of nouns and verbs that make up happy — travel, sports, someone you like to be with, someplace you like to go, and then realize we can add adjectives and adverbs to these. For example, I like reading; but what would make me happy is reading a particularbook, in a cottage by a brook, which is next to a forest, sitting by the fireside on a rocking chair, with a golden retriever by my side and so on and so forth, the list could go into paragraphs. All the things listed are external – and fuelled by desires. So I will be happy when my desires are fulfilled. But what will happen along the long journey of reaching those desires?

It's great to know where you want to go. However, it's far away. Do I want to be happy "then"?

I remember speaking to a professional mountain climber who had scaled Mount Everest, and she said it's a thrill making the climb all the days, fuelled by the desire of getting to the peak. However, coming back down is a little less exciting and when you get back home...it gets boring for the next few months with the thrill behind you.

The fulfilment of desires can only provide very short lived moments of euphoria.

So what is this clichéd happiness all about?

This book courageously takes on the question and looks at it from various angles, exploring the subject using stories, examples, and research that help you introspect and make happiness oriented changes in your life.

Aruna is one of the happier people I know. I have seen her brave problems that would have overwhelmed others, and handle them with a smile. She writes from a happy space of mind and for a book such as this, it's the best qualification.

I had gifted a galley pre-publication copy of this book to my mother. She finished it and gifted it back to me saying that I would benefit more from reading the book myself, than from publishing it.

That started my journey of picking up the book as a reader, and it helped change the way I see the world.

The book was created from a happy space, something that is reflected in the style of writing, as stories unfold to bring alive the concepts.

I trust you will enjoy it as much as I did.

Sohin Lakhani
CEO
Embassy Books

DEDICATION

To my soul-mate, my friend, philosopher and guide,
my husband – Santosh.

He has taught me how to live life.
In the twenty-one years of our association,
I have never seen him unhappy, sulky,
or depressed for more than a few minutes.
He has this unique ability of springing back to
his happy self even in the most challenging situations.

I dedicate this book to you my dear...

ACKNOWLEDGEMENTS

I am truly blessed in every sense of the word. I humbly bow to the Almighty and my Guru- *Swami Nityananda of Ganeshpuri*, and express my sincere gratitude for the blessings and the insights I received on my journey to Happiness that I could share with you.

My heartfelt thanks to all those who contributed to this book and helped turn my dream into a reality.

- My husband and best friend *Santosh*, for always being patient with me and showing me the path to happiness.

- My Parents *Pramod* and *Vijaya Agnihotri*, for the precious values you imbibed in me that set a foundation of my life. Your encouragement, support and love motivates me to put in my best in whatever I do.

- My late *Parents-in-law* for their love and blessings.

- My Publisher and dear friend *Sohin Lakhani*, for showing confidence in me as a writer. Your contribution to my writing career is invaluable. Thank you for being such an important part of my journey and writing the foreword for my book.

- My dear friends *Nazlin Lakhani*, *Sanjay Beswal*, and *Shivratan Singrodia*, for taking time out of your busy schedules, reading the galley pre-publication copy, and giving your constructive feedback.

It certainly added value to my book.

- To Team Embassy with a special mention to *Safa Punjabi* and *Samshuddin Dhaboiwala* for all your help and creative suggestions.

- To a few people who were more excited about this book than I was. *Sakina Rampurawala, Akshara KR, Parveen Sheikh*, and *Sfurti Tatkare*. Thanks for patiently listening to all the chapters I read out to you guys with interest and generous appreciation. This kept me going. I am blessed to have you all in my life.

- My friend and designer *Sonal Churi* for a fantastic cover and layout for my book, which makes the book look so 'Happy.'

- My friend and mentor *Suma Varughese* for the valuable writing lessons; and my friend *Madhu Sahoo* for always motivating me to write.

- Last but not the least I thank all my readers; because you read, I write.

TABLE OF CONTENTS

PREFACE

The memory of 17th July 2012, still sends chills down my spine. I remember the exact moment when I was checking my phone in the morning, and suddenly noticed an outpour of condolence messages for one of my Facebook friends, Rohit. When I clicked on his timeline, I was shaken to know that he had passed away the previous day. What blew me off was that he committed suicide! My first reaction was that of disbelief, 'Rohit cannot commit suicide; is this some kind of a prank!' Rohit was a doctor – young, charismatic, kind-hearted, spirited, humble, and always ready to help. He had totally impressed me in the few interactions that we had. However, the news was true. Rohit had passed away. It had been a few years since I had last met him, but did follow him on social media. He looked quite happy in the pictures that he shared. I deliberated, what made such a lovely person end his life?

When I spoke to a couple of common friends who were close to him, I learned that he was suffering from depression for the past few years and was undergoing treatment for the same. Rohit lived such a picture-perfect life that it was difficult to believe that something was going on behind the scenes.

It is highly disheartening to know that depression has become an epidemic in our modern world. The World Health Organization reports that more than 800,000 people die by suicide every year. It says, more people die from suicide than from conflicts, wars and natural disasters combined. Depression is a common and serious medical illness that negatively affects the way you feel, the way you think, and the way you act; and can affect anybody irrespective of the age, race or economic status. Depression generally makes a person feel worthless, sad and develops suicidal tendencies.

It is precisely the opposite of happiness. Happiness is a state of well-being and contentment. When a person is happy, he/she is in a peaceful, content, blissful and joyous state and has a positive outlook towards life.

We live in a world, where we are always under pressure. We are multi-tasking all the time. We have our careers, goals, family, health, and relationships to handle. It wears us down mentally and emotionally, and we start wondering, "Why am I doing all this?" and invariably the answer is, "Because I want to be happy." However, we realize that happiness is lost in the struggle, pain, and the challenges that we go through.

So the more significant question is, "Can one still be happy while facing the struggles and experiencing pain and grief?"

My journey in pursuit of happiness started with this question. I also went through my share of worry, anxiety, depression, insecurity, struggling to make sense of life and its meaning. However, my life took a magical turn when I stepped on the spiritual path. I am grateful that I met a lot of wise people on my journey, whose contribution was humongous in moulding me into a person I am today.

Once I asked a spiritual teacher I met, "I want to be happy and peaceful in life. What should I do?" He answered with a smile, "It's easy. Look at everything in life as an observer. Remember, you are neither the doer nor the experiencer. You are a mere spectator of the phenomenon called life."

What he said was very profound, but I had a hard time making sense of it at that stage in my life. I found it very difficult to separate myself from my emotions, thoughts, experiences, and actions. I realized that I was too attached to all of them and hence could not view them in perspective.

It took me almost a decade of inner exploration to understand this profound yet simple truth. It was a roller coaster ride when on some days I found myself beaming with happiness while on others, I was down in the dumps. However, gradually I was moving in the right direction - in that of my goal. Through various sessions of introspection, meditation and multiple learnings, I discovered that what I was searching for was well within me, and so I started finding out ways to reach there.

When I began to look at life as an observer, I could view all the problems and challenges from a distance, and that reduced their intensity. It also gave me the space to address them in a better way. This practice reduced my miseries, sufferings, and unhappiness to a great extent, and I began to look at life from a very different perspective. It brought a significant shift in my attitude, my thoughts, and my actions.

I understood that happiness is our basic nature and how it slowly gets marred by negative conditioning and limiting beliefs as we grow up. I learned that happiness is unconditional, and one can stay happy even under the most challenging circumstances. Viewing life from an observer's standpoint gave me the clarity on when, why and how I slip into any negative emotion. Through my experiences and understanding, I also found out ways to bounce back to a happy state again.

The idea of writing this book came to me when I witnessed the eternal struggles of the people around me, trying to make sense of life and the challenges it entails, like I once did. Few appalling incidences shook me to the core - A teenager boy in our neighbourhood jumped from the 14th floor of his building and committed suicide, without any apparent reason; My best friend's daughter went into depression and stopped going to college as she could not handle the stress; A constant unrest in my neighbour's house as the daughter-in-law and mother-in-law could not get along; A single mother I know of going through her challenges while also taking care of her ailing mother all by herself.

I thought, if I have gone through my share of tough times and have learned to bounce back and stay in a happy state while passing through them, I should share it with the world. In the process, I found specific tools that could help me get in touch with my happy self by changing my state of mind. They are not rocket science, but simple things that we tend to overlook.

The Happiness Manual is an attempt to help you handle any challenge in your life gracefully, with a smile on your face. This book has 21 ways (tools that I learned) to stay happy which you can reach out to, in your difficult times. There are examples from my life and that from the experiences of people around me, some popular stories, fables, and folklore in this book that makes it an interesting read, has a more significant impact and renders a higher understanding.

You may keep this book handy, and whenever you feel that you are digressing from the path of happiness, you can randomly open a chapter and start reading it. I can say with certainty, that it will change your state of mind to a happy one.

Each chapter concludes with,

Reflections - the gist of the chapter,

Step to happiness - a practical idea/tool to reach the happy state

Happiness mantra - a powerful positive statement, which if repeated continuously in your mind will have the desired impact.

Every happiness mantra starts with a "just for today...." If you commit yourself to anything only for a single day, it becomes less overwhelming and reduces the fear and worry of achieving it. Thus your goals seem achievable and within your reach.

So, take life one day at a time.

May you discover the 'Happy You' and make this world a happy place.

Aruna Joshi

Mumbai

WHAT IS HAPPINESS?

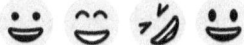

Life is an amazing expedition, where events are beautifully orchestrated to teach us lessons we need to learn. Sometimes the lessons are subtle, sometimes plainly obvious but they help us by revealing the larger perspective that we may tend to overlook.

This incident occurred a few months back. It was one of those days when everything was going tangential to what I had planned, lowering my spirits - I woke up to a water shortage in my apartment complex, my domestic help did not turn up, my laptop developed some problem and the screen went blank...everything suddenly demanded my urgent attention.

I was already running late for a meeting scheduled for 12.00 noon at Nariman Point, which is about 40km from where I live. I decided to take a train instead of driving down through the heavy traffic in Mumbai. It was one of the hottest days of summer. The Sun was bright and burning. After I finished my meeting I had no energy left to walk back to the station. I looked around for a taxi. The road wore a deserted look and I was relieved to see a solitary cab standing further down the road. I walked up to the cab and asked the driver if he would take me to the station, which was about 1.5 km from there. The cab-driver seemed to be in no mood to go and said, "Madam, I am waiting for a long-distance passenger." His reply irritated me, and I walked away to wait for another cab. I waited for a while, but there was no sign of any other cab in that area. When the heat became unbearable, I went back to the cab-driver hesitantly and requested him to drive me to the station. This time he obliged, and I quickly got into the taxi, before he could change his mind.

As we headed towards the station, he got talking, "Ma'am I know you got irritated when I said no. But you know why I refused to drive you to the station?"

I looked up and gave him a 'who cares' kind of look and began checking my mobile phone. Ignoring my expression which he could see from the rear-view mirror, he continued, "I am from a village in Utter Pradesh. My wife is in the hospital battling for her life. I sent whatever money I had for her treatment this morning; but I just received a call from the doctor saying that she may not survive for long. And now I have no money left to buy a ticket to reach my village and be with my wife during her last moments." Pausing for a moment, he added, "So, I thought, if I could get a long-distance passenger, I could earn at least 500 rupees which can buy me a train ticket to reach there."

I was stunned by what he said.

"So, Ma'am please don't misunderstand me." He further added, "Since you were standing in the hot sun and looked very uncomfortable, I relented to your request."

Every word he said seemed genuine. Listening to his heart-wrenching story, my eyes welled up. I asked him, "So, who is there with your wife now?"

"My 70-year-old mother and my two little daughters, and they are all crying Ma'am. I feel so helpless." He said, trying hard to stop his tears from rolling down. I was numbed by this conversation. I came back to my senses when he said, "Ma'am the station is right here and your fair is 25 rupees please."

I put my hand in my wallet, took out whatever cash I had, kept 50 rupees for my return trip home and handed over the rest of the cash to the cab driver.

"Ma'am its 2500 rupees!" he exclaimed,

I said, "Brother, this is the least I can do. Please take the next possible train to your village and be with your wife."

"Ma'am, thank you so much. But please take my mobile number. I will return every penny when I come back." Tears of joy and relief were flowing from his eyes.

My heart felt heavy and words refused to flow out of my mouth. I signaled him not to worry about it and waved him good-bye. Turning around, I wiped away the tears about to roll down my cheeks. His story had touched me deeply. As I silently walked towards the station, I experienced absolute stillness in my being, even as I cut through the thick noisy crowd. The things that I was fretting about since morning had disappeared from my mind. No complaints. No qualms. Only gratitude and peace prevailed in its place.

I could not forget the expression of joy on the cab-driver's face when he unexpectedly got the money he so badly needed to reach his ailing wife. It was priceless! The feeling that I could help somebody – a total stranger whom I may never meet again, was magical. The whole incident left me feeling good about myself and my existence.

The profound serenity that comes with an act of altruism is a source of real joy and happiness. The thought and the act of helping others gives a momentary purpose to our lives, and fulfilling that, leaves an ever-lasting impression on our soul. Focusing too much on ourselves often induces a lot of stress and unhappiness. But these kinds of incidents ignite compassion, empathy and kindness within us. When these feelings take over, we become centred, our energy is directed towards helping others, and we stop thinking about ourselves. However, the biggest advantage of selfless acts is that we are not only making the other person happy by making a difference in his life, but we also feel uplifted and happy ourselves. The incident described above certainly added value to my life and left me feeling more grateful than ever before. The feeling of being able to help a stranger brought in an indescribable sense of peace, contentment and happiness.

Matthieu Ricard, a Tibetan Buddhist monk who has been called 'the world's happiest man', says, "If your mind is filled with benevolence, passion and solidarity, it is a very healthy state of mind that is conducive to flourishing." He further adds, "So you, yourself, are in a much better mental state. Your body will be healthier. And also, people will perceive it as something nice."

What is happiness?

In philosophy - 'Happiness translates the Greek concept of Eudaimonia, and refers to a good life, or flourishing, rather than simply an emotion.'

In psychology - 'Happiness is a mental or emotional state of overall well-being which can be defined by, among others, positive or pleasant emotions ranging from contentment to intense joy.'

Even as small children, we very well understand and experience the emotions that fall in the spectrum of happiness such as peace, joy, faith, and love; as those are our inherent characteristics. But as we grow up, our focus grows outwards and so do our needs and wants. We get introduced to various other emotions such as hate, anger, fear, jealousy, sadness etc. We fall prey to competition, comparison, greed, desires and eventually become unhappy.

Is it possible to return to the happy state which is our intrinsic nature?

Let us look at it this way.

You buy an ornamented, glittery brass vase and leave it unattended for a few months. Slowly the vase gets tarnished and the shine starts to wear off. What do you do then? You figure out how to remove the stains and restore the vase to its former beauty.

We are like that shining vase – happy and joyful. Eventually we get covered by various layers of negative emotions, and beliefs that destroy our true state i.e. happiness. We need to find out ways to remove the erosion and stains. As soon as we do that we are that shining vase again.

The process of getting back to the happy state requires some work on ourselves; better understanding of life, unlearning certain things that we've learnt, developing the right attitude and virtues, clearing the mental clutter, and removing the layers of false beliefs and doubts wrapped around us.

This book gives you 21 ways to regain the happy state, no matter what!

ARE YOU REALLY HAPPY?

However ridiculous it may sound, our upbringing was against the expression of an overt sense of happiness with almost a caution to it as if to say, "Don't be so happy or you will soon have to be sad," "Don't laugh too much or you will have to cry." Well, as a child you believe whatever is told to you is true. These beliefs stayed with me for a very long time. They shaped my nature and my demeanour. For the longest time, I was scared to express my joy. When I achieved something or was happy and wanted to announce my accomplishments and joy to the world, my belief would peep out from deep within me and say, "Hey, don't do that or you will soon become sad." When I was with friends, we shared a joke, and I wanted to laugh out loud, my deep-rooted belief would only allow me to smile.

Slowly I turned into a quiet and serious-minded person. I didn't know what dancing with joy and roaring with laughter was! People would often mistake my quietness for sadness. Even if I was happy, it did not reflect on my being. Since my thoughts and actions were not in sync, it gave rise to conflict within. The result was that my happiness was short-lived. It imposed restrictions on my capacity to take risks and live up to my highest potential. I started living out of fear and was unhappy most of the times.

In the later years of my life, only when I became more aware of the universal processes, started understanding life and went on the path of self-discovery, could I change my beliefs about happiness. It did involve a lot of inner work, understanding, faith, and acceptance, but in the end, I was successful.

Every human being is striving hard to achieve happiness. All our actions are directed towards the ultimate goal, i.e. happiness. We study hard, get a good job, earn money, get married, and start a family...all with the hope of achieving happiness. However, there is something amiss. If we are working so hard to achieve happiness, why is there despondency all over? Why are so many people being treated for depression? Why are the suicide rates increasing day by day? If we reflect on our lives, we will find,

Today we live in a world of greater comfort and more wealth, but still, find ourselves complaining and whining about things around us.

We have become intellectually mature but emotionally weaker.

We have many friends on social networking platforms, but struggle to maintain close relationships.

We pay more attention to our outer safety and security but are highly insecure from within.

We chase big things in life but in the process forget the simple things that bring joy.

Before you read any further, I urge you to pause and reflect on the question, "Are you really happy?" You may take the following test to know your happiness quotient.

Answer the following questions in a 'YES' or 'NO.'

I like to be in control of everything in my life.

☐ YES   ☐ NO

I often do things to please others.

☐ YES   ☐ NO

I like to possess the latest electronic gadgets.

☐ YES   ☐ NO

I am afraid to be vulnerable.

☐ YES   ☐ NO

I hate child-like behavior.

☐ YES   ☐ NO

I am a perfectionist.

☐ YES   ☐ NO

I get easily stressed out when the deadlines are not met.

☐ YES   ☐ NO

I form an opinion about somebody in the first meeting itself.
☐ YES   ☐ NO

When I do things for others, I expect the same from them.

☐ YES   ☐ NO

I feel I am unworthy of certain things in life.

☐ YES   ☐ NO

I can't easily forgive the people who have hurt me.

☐ YES   ☐ NO

I feel I am the unfortunate one.

☐ YES   ☐ NO

I feel jealous when someone undeserving gets more than I do.

☐ YES   ☐ NO

I can't easily trust people.

☐ YES   ☐ NO

I often worry about the future.

☐ YES   ☐ NO

When things go wrong in my life, I easily tend to give up.

☐ YES   ☐ NO

I always tend to come across negative people.

☐ YES   ☐ NO

I often don't take steps due to the fear of failure.

☐ YES ☐ NO

I believe people talk bad things behind my back.

☐ YES ☐ NO

I often indulge in negative self-talk.

☐ YES ☐ NO

If all the answers to the above questions are a 'NO', then you don't need this book. However, if the majority of answers are a 'YES', then I urge you to read further. I can assure you that if you read and follow the tips mentioned in this book with utmost sincerity, you will have unlocked all the doors to a 'happier you.' Then if you retake this test, your result may change drastically.

IN PURSUIT OF HAPPINESS

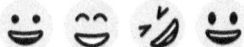

*"If you think sunshine brings you happiness
then you haven't danced in the rains."*

- Unknown -

My friend Geeta narrated a beautiful incident from her life. This happened on a hot sunny day when the temperature in Mumbai had touched 40 degrees Celsius, and Geeta was returning home from her job in the afternoon that day. The heat was unbearable, and she took shelter under a bus-stop roof as she waited for the bus to arrive. At a distance, she saw an old woman struggling with some bags in her hands while trying to cover her face at the same time from the scorching Sun, as she walked towards the sheltering shade of the bus stop. Geeta went towards her with a smile and helped her reach the shade.

The old woman asked her, "Do we know each other?"

Geeta replied, "No we don't. Why do you ask that?"

"Because you smiled and helped me." The old woman said.

"Do we really need to know each other to smile and help? Isn't it enough that we are fellow-beings?" The old woman was so touched by this unexpected reply that she hugged Geeta and thanked her, and both their faces wore a happy smile.

Happiness is so simple. An unpretentious smile coming from the heart and a genuine intention to help someone can do wonders. Making someone happy is a sure-shot way to your own happiness.

Perfect happiness may mean different things to different people. For some it may be spending peaceful time with their loved ones; for some it may be experiencing deep peace and calm in the lap of nature, like a long walk on a starry night, or listening to the harmonious sound of waves by the seashore, or scaling up the mountain peaks; for some it could be an event that they looked forward to, such as marriage, birth of a child, visiting a dream destination, winning a tournament, getting a place in their chosen career; for some it could be achieving their goals; or for some it could be showing kindness, compassion, empathy, love etc.

Whatever the definition of happiness is, in all the above examples there are a few common threads. In those moments of happiness:

- You experience harmony, as your inner world and outer world are in sync,

- You feel your internal conflicts dissolving,

- You experience being in the present moment with no thoughts of the past or the future,

- You experience immense peace and contentment,

- You are in an absolute healthy state of well-being.

Happiness is an inner state of being, but unfortunately, we look for it outside and get disappointed. We are saddened if things don't go as planned, or if people deceive us, or if they don't behave as we wish them to behave. However, the truth is that the world outside is illusory and beyond our control. What we can control is only our mind. We always have a choice to stay happy or unhappy, irrespective of the external conditions and circumstances.

1

Happiness is by Choice, Not by Chance

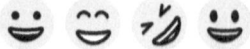

Maya is a caregiver. When my mother-in-law was confined to bed due to a stroke combined with an advanced stage of Alzheimer's, Maya stepped into our lives and took charge of the situation. She would enter our house every morning and greet us with a big grin and an enthusiastic 'Good Morning' as if she were meeting her loved ones after a long time. Her enthusiasm was contagious, magically changing the energy of our house. All through the day, even while doing the filthiest of tasks like changing the diapers and cleaning, we could hear her humming tunes from old Hindi movies. Maya seemed happy in her space, and she radiated that happiness all through the house.

Being a writer and a keen observer of human behavioral patterns, her conduct intrigued me. I was curious to know more about her and her secret to happiness. However, what I learned left me flabbergasted. She had two children, one of who was deaf and dumb, and the other was mentally challenged. Her husband was an alcoholic, and there was no support of any kind from her parents or in-laws.

I could not refrain myself from asking her, "Despite all these issues in your life, how do you manage to maintain such a positive demeanour and keep smiling all the time?"

She said, "All these challenges in my personal life give me an opportunity to understand other people's problems better. I can empathise with them, and this helps me do my job well. When I step out of my house every morning, I tell myself, 'Maya, you have two choices – carry your problems to work or leave them behind to handle when you get back.' And I choose the second."

I was stunned by her reply. The wisdom that came from this so-called illiterate woman was incredible. Maya exercised her choice to stay happy in spite of all the challenges she faced.

If we wait for conditions to be ideal to make us happy, our wait will be eternal. In life, there are always ups and downs, challenging situations, duties to be performed, responsibilities to be borne, health concerns, relationship issues, financial problems, and so on. However challenging they may seem, none of these conditions can stop us from being happy. Then what does? It is all us! We put those conditions that prevent us from being happy and then we blame everybody and everything for our unhappiness. For example, "How can I be happy if I don't have enough money?" or "My mother-in-law treats me badly and you still expect me to be happy?"

This happens because we link our happiness to certain conditions and it fluctuates accordingly.

However, it does help to understand and accept that all challenges and issues are external, whereas happiness is internal. It is we who give away our power to those external things and let them control our happiness. But there is also an important point here we cannot overlook, and that is, we have a choice, to give away or retain that power.

Happiness is affected by the choice or choices we make. And if the authority to choose rests with us, why can't we consciously choose to be happy?

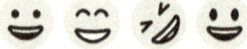

There is a famous story of the Buddha and an angry man. When the Buddha was teaching a group of people, a bystander who was angry due to some reason started hurling abuses at him. The Buddha patiently waited for a while until the man was done and asked the group and the man with a smiling face, "If you gift something to your friend and he does not accept it, who would then own the gift, you or your friend?"

"I would own the gift," said one person and everyone nodded in agreement. "Isn't it obvious?" added the angry stranger.

"Absolutely right," said the Buddha, "So whenever someone tries to abuse or unload their anger on you, you have a choice, either to accept or reject it, to own or disown it, to get affected or unaffected by it."

Similarly, in any given situation we always have a choice – the choice of being happy or unhappy. Happiness is a state of mind, and it just takes a moment to alter that. Well, it may seem like an oversimplified statement. As human beings, we all are subjected to various challenging emotional, mental and physical conditions many times in our lives. Many people struggle with depression, anxiety, and stress. And in such situations, to tell someone, 'alter your mind to a state of happiness' may not work. To be able to achieve a state of joy and maintain it all the time, would entail a lot of work from us. It would require us to make multiple choices – the choice to accept the situation, the choice to take responsibility, the choice to turn the situation in our favour, and the choice to be happy. We need to continually remind ourselves of the powerful beings that we are and the power to choose that has been bestowed upon us. If we remember to exercise this choice, we can remain in a state of happiness all the time.

Reflections:
Our happiness depends on us. We can be as happy as we choose to be. It is a freewill given to us that we need to exercise. However difficult the situation may be, nobody can stop us from being happy, but we ourselves.

Step to Happiness:
Whenever any situation arises, that makes you unhappy, dissociate from the situation and tell yourself, "It is just an experience that I am going through, and it is transient. I have been bestowed with the power of choice. I exercise this power and choose to be happy."

Happiness Mantra:
Just for today, I consciously choose to be happy at every moment and in every given situation.

2

The Power of Empathy

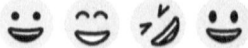

I recently heard a heart-warming story on empathy narrated by a friend. It goes like this.

Once there lived a farmer in a small village, who worked fingers to the bone to provide for his family. One year there was a drought, and the farmer was left with no choice than to sell his puppies. He felt terrible that he had to do this, but he had no way out. He painted an advertising board and set about to nail it on the pole on his fence. As he was punching the last nail on the board, he felt a jerk on his slightly long shirt he was wearing. He turned around and saw a little boy with an innocent face, trying to reach him.

"Sir, I would like to buy one of your puppies," the little boy said.

"Well son, these puppies are a good breed and they cost much money," said the farmer thinking that the boy might go away.

The boy seemed to be disappointed momentarily. He then put his hand deep in his pocket and removed some coins and said, "Look, I've got thirty-nine cents. Is that enough to take a look at the puppies?"

"Sure," said the farmer.

He whistled and called out loud, "Zoya, come here."

From the doghouse, came out Zoya followed by four little balls of fur down the ramp in a style as if participating in a fashion show.

The little boy was so delighted to see them that he started clapping with happiness. As the dog and the four puppies approached the fence where the farmer and the boy were standing, the boy saw some movement happening in the doghouse. As he waited to see what was happening, he saw another fur ball struggling to come out on the ramp and walking and stumbling towards the fence with great difficulty.

"I want that one," the little boy said, pointing towards the last puppy.

Moving his hand over the boy's head, the farmer said, "Why do you want that puppy. He cannot even walk. He will not be able to play and run with you like other dogs."

At this, the little boy reached down and began rolling up one leg of his trousers. As he was doing this, the farmer noticed a steel brace running down both sides of his leg to a specially made shoe. Then looking up to the farmer the little boy said, "You see sir, even I don't run so well myself, and he needs someone who understands him."

Being empathetic means merely being able to see the world through somebody else's eyes. It applies to pain and pleasure both. Feeling the pain and sadness of others around you makes you an empathetic person.

What people naturally crave for is to be understood by others. Most often we do the exact opposite. We judge them, form opinions and label them. However, if we can see the situation from their perspective, their behaviour will seem justified.

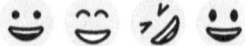

Being empathetic helps you understand the other person better. You may even feel the pain that he/she is going through in life. Being kind and caring comes easily to you if you are an empath.

Once, on the streets of Kolkata, Mother Teresa came across a young woman lying in the gutter in front of a hospital. The woman was so sick that she did not even notice that rats and cockroaches were feeding on her feet. Mother picked her up and took her to the hospital requesting them to admit her. However, she was refused admission because she was poor, and was very sick.

The epitome of kindness that she was, her heart broke, and she carried the woman back to the street, and there, she stayed with the woman for hours until she died. Mother Teresa felt like no one should have to die alone, forgotten and in despair on the dirty street.

Post that she lived a life of kindness, committing to help people, feeding, nursing, caring for the sick and differently abled people. This undaunted act of hers brought a smile on the face of a person who was dying.

Being empathetic certainly makes you feel happy. You feel good about yourself because you could understand others, and other people also feel happy that there is someone who understands them.

So if anytime you feel that you have drifted from the happy state of mind, being empathetic can bring you back to that state again.

Reflections:
Empathy is one of the most potent characteristics you can have.
It helps you to see the world from other person's perspective and
enables you to understand life and people around you in a more
profound sense.

Step to Happiness:
Only when you empathise with people around, you will
understand the true nature of happiness. Try not to judge them.
Put yourselves in their shoes before reacting. Be a good listener
and try to feel what the other person is feeling. This way you will
be able to better connect with everyone around you.

Happiness Mantra:
Just for today, I will try to understand others in an
unprejudiced way.

3

Attitude Defines Happiness

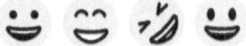

Baby mosquito came back after his first flying experience. His dad asked him, "How did you feel?" He replied, "It was wonderful Daddy... All humans clapped their hands for me".

It is our perspective of looking at things and situations that matter.

One of my favourite things to do is observe people and study their behaviours and reactions. While writing this book, I was determined to find out what makes people happy and the difference between the happy and not so happy people. And the primary differentiating factor I found was 'Attitude'. Our attitude defines our reaction to a situation, and this reaction, in turn, determines our happiness. Our attitude towards life in general, or towards any situation, in particular, is the barometer of our happiness.

I know of an old couple that exude happiness all the time. One can feel the positive and happy vibes on entering their house. I look forward to visiting them and love to be in their company. I use to always wonder what makes them so likable. Well, I got to know the secret when I was once invited to their house for dinner. I was welcomed with a warm and cheerful greeting as I entered. The table was neatly arranged with a variety of food, and the room was filled with appetizing aromas of the type of food the old lady cooked. As we all sat to eat, and as I took my first bite of the vegetable, my expressions changed. It had excess salt. Seeing the expressions on my face, the lady realized the problem and profusely apologized. Before I could say anything, the old man intervened. He said, "You know, my wife is the best cook in the world. When I travelled extensively during my working years, I can't tell you how much I missed the delicious food cooked by her, and how I would wait to come back home." He continued, "This particular vegetable tastes too good with rice. Try it, and it will just balance the salt." What a graceful way of handling a situation! It saved his wife from further embarrassment. The situation which could have gone in a negative spiral beautifully spun into a positive one. And all of us happily finished our dinner.

There are two ways of dealing with any situation, and both ways will take us in entirely different directions. The result can be happy or unhappy. It totally on depends our attitude which way we choose to go.

Have you seen happy people? How do they look? They have a smile on their face, they look contended, they exude positive energy, they are very comfortable and happy with themselves, they are ready to laugh and have fun, whatever the situation may be. *They also go through their share of problems and sufferings, but they learn the art of untangling happiness from that suffering.*

There is a story of a king whose kingdom was going through a lot of unrest. The king was curious to find out the reason. He decided to do an experiment. He told his minister to place a big boulder in the middle of the road and he hid behind the bush as he wanted to see the reaction of the people who passed through that road. Some of the wealthiest merchants and courtiers came by and just walked around it, loudly blaming the king for not keeping the streets clear, but none did anything about getting the big stone out of the way. After a while, a peasant passed from there carrying a load of

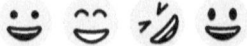

vegetables. On seeing the boulder lying in the middle of the road, the peasant laid down his burden and tried to move the stone to the side of the road. After great difficulty, he finally succeeded. As the peasant picked up his load of vegetables, he noticed a purse lying in the road where the boulder had been. The purse was filled with gold coins and a note from the king saying that the gold was for the person who removed the boulder from the roadway.

This is the power of attitude. The poor peasant did not sit and whine and complain and wait for anybody else to do it. He took the responsibility and removed the stone himself and got rewarded for his positive attitude.

Two people were asked, "What is rainfall?"

One person replied, "Rainfall is the result of water vapour condensing and precipitating, forming droplets that fall from clouds due to gravity. It is an important part of the water cycle."

The other person said, "Rainfall is the most beautiful phenomenon of nature, it's a miracle how the droplets of water fall from the sky wetting the parched earth, enlivening the flora and the fauna and stimulating growth."

If you choose to look at everything that happens in your life through a lens of wonderment and miracle, you will always be happy in life.

Reflections:
Our attitude defines where we are and where we will reach
in our life. Our attitude shapes up our reality. It defines our
happiness. If we look at everything that happens in our life
through the lens of positivity, it will empower us and make us
successful and happy.

Step to Happiness:
Remember that there
are different perspectives
of looking at the same
situation. The perspective
will determine our
attitude. So why not
adopt an outlook that will
make us and everybody
around us happy.

Happiness Mantra:
Just for today, I
will keep a positive
attitude.

4

Fear Cripples Happiness While Courage Propels it

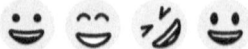

Lucius Annaeus Seneca, a Roman Philosopher, once said, "Where fear is, happiness is not." It is our perspective of looking at things and situations that matter.

When you are able to transcend fear, the happiness that you feel is irreplaceable. I experienced this a few years back on one of those monsoon days.

I had signed up for water rappelling adventure camp, held at a breathtakingly beautiful location near Mumbai. Such events take place when the monsoon is at its peak. Rappelling is a method of a quick and safe descend after a climb. It's an act of descending a mountain face by sliding down a rope, which is attached to a body harness and fastened to an overhead projection. Sufficient friction is provided to make the speed of descent controllable. Rappelling through the waterfall is far more adventurous than normal rappelling, with a guaranteed rush of heavy adrenaline through you. In water rappelling, the support of the rock is only for a few feet; after which the descent is supposed to be through the waterfall away from the rock.

"Go! What are you waiting for?" my trainer commanded in a rather stern voice.

"No, I can't! I am scared." I screamed.

My body was hanging in mid-air, parallel to the ground at the height of 100 feet. The only anchor was my feet resting on the slippery rock and the rope that I was holding on tightly with both hands.

We, a group of twenty people had trekked our way to the top of the old Buddhist caves where the water rappelling camp was set. A thick white milky waterfall was formed as the water surged through the mountains, gushing over the rock edge. We had to descend through this waterfall to the base.

"You must go now. There are two more people to go after you, and we need to wind up before the weather gets too bad." The trainer shouted.

From our group, seventeen people had already finished their rappelling. I chose to go towards the end. Not a very adventurous person at heart, I had enrolled in this programme, only on the insistence of my friends. Since I had acrophobia (fear of heights), I thought I might gather some courage looking at others do it.

I stood there on the top, waiting for my turn, geared with a climbing harness that ensured my safety. Despite this, I was so scared that I wished the weather got really bad and the event got aborted. But nothing of that sort happened. When the trainer announced my name, my heart leaped out of my chest.

"No, I can't do this. I have a fear of heights. I will die!" I shouted at the top of my voice so that it could reach the trainer through the roaring sound of the waterfall. This was a highly challenging task for me. And even if I gathered my guts to rappel down, I was certain that I will die of suffocation (my second fear) in the waterfall. "I am such a fool to have put my life in jeopardy," I thought.

As I was battling with two of my grave fears, I heard a voice from within say, *'You can do it! This is your opportunity to beat your fears. Do it now or you will never be able to do it.'*

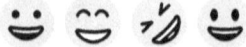

This motivating voice from within gave me the courage and confidence to jump off the cliff, silencing my fear for a few moments. The next thing I remember is descending the 100 feet high cliff through the dense waterfall. I was completely breathless and shivering as I came down through ice cold water. Within a few minutes, I safely landed at the base, received by another trainer from the crew.

As soon as I landed, I pinched myself to make sure that I was still in my mortal body and had not already turned into a free spirit. When I looked around, my friends were standing there, cheering for me. "You did it, girl! We are so proud of you!" They came and hugged me. I couldn't believe that I actually did water rappelling. I told myself, "Hey look, you are safe. You could do it! There is nothing to be scared of now." It was indeed an ecstatic moment. I proudly posed for a picture, with a glorious smile. It was one of the most incredible and happiest moments of my life.

I had had a rendezvous with two of my greatest fears, and I could transcend them. Had I not done it then, I would have probably never mustered the courage to reach to the top of the rock again. I felt something shift within me.

One of our biggest enemies preventing us from realizing our true potential and happiness is our fears. Fears are like demons working inside of us, paralysing us emotionally, mentally, and physically. They sabotage our power, strength, and zest to achieve what we want, depriving us of the success and happiness that we truly deserve.

How does one deal with these fears? The best way to do this is to face them and transcend them. Until we transcend them, they will keep on disempowering us. It is said, 'Your greatest success lies beyond your greatest fears.' Whenever we get an opportunity to transcend our fears, the demons will come with a mighty force to pull us back. They have the power to captivate our being and prevent you from taking a step. And we tend to find some excuse or procrastinate. But the secret to transcending the fear is to face it. Gather all the strength and courage and simply take the first step towards fear. Happiness will surely follow.

Reflections:
Happiness is often crippled by fear. We live in the anticipation that something will go wrong and hence we let go of many opportunities that could take our lives to a different level. Our happiness is hidden in the closet of fear. Let open the closet and let happiness out.

Step to Happiness:
The best way to deal with fear is to face it. A little push and inspiration are required to take that step towards your fear. Draw that inspiration, gather the courage and take that step. You will never regret it.

Happiness Mantra:
Just for today, I will act out of courage.

5

Comparison Steals Joy

During your growing up years, when you have a lesser understanding of life, you tend to fall into the comparison trap. As a young girl, I used to complain to my mother, "Mom, look Shriya rides a scooter and I have a bicycle," "Ritu's parents give her permission for night-outs, and you and dad are so strict with me." I used to feel my friends are leading a happier life. After repeatedly listening to my complaints and arguments, one day my mum made me sit and told me a story that stayed with me till date.

There was once a crow, who lived in the forest and was very happy with his life. One day while he was happily flying in the jungle, he saw a swan; and a thought crossed his mind, "This swan is sparkling white, and I am jet black. This swan must be the happiest bird in the world."

He decided to go and share this with the swan. "Actually," the swan replied, "I felt that I was the happiest bird around until I saw a parrot, which has two colours. I now think the parrot is the happiest bird in the entire universe."

The crow then approached the parrot. The parrot explained, "I lived a very happy life until I saw a peacock. I have only two colours, but the peacock has multiple colours."

The crow thought that there was a point. He went to the zoo to meet the peacock and saw that hundreds of people had gathered to see him. The crow now had no doubts that peacock is the happiest bird in the world – he is beautiful and is also getting so much of attention and appreciation. After the people left, the crow approached the peacock and said, "Dear peacock, you look so beautiful. People flock around you to get the glimpse of your beauty. When people see me, they immediately shoo me away. I think you must be the happiest bird on the planet."

The peacock replied, "I also thought that I was the most beautiful and happy bird on the planet. However, because of my beauty, I am entrapped in this zoo and have lost my freedom. I thought a lot over it and realized that crow is the only bird that is not kept in the cage. So for past few days I have been thinking that if I were a crow, I could happily roam everywhere."

Isn't our problem precisely like the crow? We compare ourselves with others without valuing what we have and become sad. We thus get entrapped in the vicious cycle of unhappiness. Comparing ourselves with others and thinking that we lack somewhere often takes us through the roller-coaster of emotions such as anger, jealousy, depression, and so on. It also lowers our self-esteem and builds in an inferiority complex. We then start focusing on what we don't have instead of what we are blessed with.

There is a famous saying, "I cried because I had no shoes until I met a man who had no feet."

In this world, 'disparity' is a common phenomenon. Some people are going to have less while some are going to have more than us. Comparing with others takes us onto the downward spiral landing into self-doubt. Mark Twain said that "Comparison is the death of joy." Usually, when we compare ourselves with the other person,

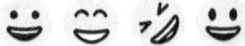

we don't have behind the scene reality of that person; so what we are comparing is our actual reality with the distorted reality of the other person.

When we see a lot of happy posts and pictures on Facebook and other social media sites, somewhere we tend to compare ourselves with them, and feel sad that we are unable to do or enjoy as much as the other person is. My friend Seth once told me a story about one of his college friends Jackie who is also his friend on FB. Seth had not met him personally post-college but regularly followed him on FB. Jackie used to post photos showing his luxuries apartment, his achievements, and pictures from his foreign tours and so on. Seth always compared himself with his friend and felt disappointed for having not been able to achieve as much in life. Seth happened to meet him once when he was in Bangalore for some work. He told me later, "Five minutes of my meeting with my friend Jackie shattered my illusion about him. Jackie was crestfallen. He was on the verge of divorce and stayed out of home most of the time, working till late hours. He had taken to alcohol and smoking."

"From that day on," Seth said, "I took a pledge that I am not going to compare myself with anybody whatsoever. And after this decision, I am a happier person."

If comparison is going to be your criteria for self-evaluation, you will always be disappointed. There will never be a point when you are better in every way than others. Instead of trying to be like others why not focus on what we are good at and excel in that. Each one of us is bestowed with some exceptional talent or quality.

Why not grow that and focus on achieving our goals, instead of wasting time and energy in comparing with others.

People, who are satisfied with what they have, and focus on their own life, are the happiest people in the world.

Reflections:
Comparison completely kills the joy out of everything. It makes us blind to the precious gifts we have and prompts us to focus on our lack. It puts us on the negative edge of life, taking us closer to our downfall. Comparison takes us far away from being happy.

Step to Happiness:
It's simple. If you want to be happy in life, stop comparing with anybody around. Every person is walking his/her path, and no two people or situations can be alike. There is beauty in the uniqueness.

 *Happiness Mantra:*
Just for today, I will appreciate my unique self and count my blessings.

6

Passion is Oxygen for the Soul

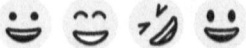

There was a young boy who was a violin prodigy. He had a natural flair for it and whenever he played violin, he would completely lose himself in the act. Once while he was walking down the street he chanced upon a famous violin teacher. He could not believe that he was standing in front of the most revered person in that field. He stopped the great teacher and asked him if he could play violin in front of him. He also thought to himself that he would give up his dream career if the teacher didn't approve of it.

The teacher agreed and he started playing. As he did so, he got so absorbed in the act, and when he finished, he was certain he'd given the most electrifying and the best performance of his life. But the ace maestro silently shook his head sadly and said, "You lack the fire."

The young man was devastated by this reply. He returned home and announced to his family about his intention of giving up his ambition. Instead he started his own business. He worked hard and soon achieved great heights.

Almost a decade later while he was on a business trip to another city he accidentally met the same teacher again. He immediately went near him and said, "I am sorry to stop you like this. I am sure you don't remember me. But I had stopped you on the street years ago to play my violin for you, and I want to thank you. Because of your advice, I abandoned my greatest love, the violin. Though it was painful, I don't regret it now because today I am enjoying great success in business. I owe all to you. But I always wanted to ask you how did you know I didn't have what it takes? How did you know all those years ago that I lacked the fire?"

The great teacher shook his head sadly and said, "You don't understand. I tell everyone who plays the violin for me that they lack the fire. If you had the fire, you wouldn't have listened."

Passion is an intense desire to do or achieve something irrespective of anybody's approval. It is an act where you easily lose yourself. It is something that you generally have a knowing of, or sometimes you may discover it accidentally. But once it is discovered, it becomes oxygen for the soul. You cannot live without it.

There goes a story of Socrates and his disciple. Once a young man came to Socrates and casually mentioned, "O great Socrates, I come to you for knowledge."

The philosopher took the young man down to the sea, waded in with him, and then dunked him under the water for thirty seconds. When he let the young man up for air, Socrates asked him to repeat what he wanted.

"Knowledge, only O' great one," he sputtered. Socrates put him under the water again, this time a little longer. After repeated dipping and responses, the philosopher asked, "what do you want"? The young man finally gasped, "Air; I want air!"

"Good," answered Socrates. "Now, when you want knowledge as much as you wanted air, you shall have it."

It is said that if you want something very intensely, you will achieve it. There is that fire burning beneath the outer layers we all are wearing. There is a fervent desire to do something or achieve

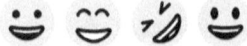

something in all of us. We all have it but most of us ignore it. The reasons could be many – self-doubt, disapproval from the people around, low self-esteem, lack of confidence, insecurity, fear etc. All these are also the roadblocks to success.

If you are passionate about something and follow it, you transcend to a different plane. Your life gains a deeper meaning. You become so happy and contended in that zone that trivial things stop affecting you. Your entire energy gets focused towards your passion. Time can't bind you any longer. Criticism, sarcasm or negative remarks do not affect a truly passionate person. It is a beautiful space to be in.

Sometimes we clearly know our passion, and sometimes we need to probe and find out while sometimes it is revealed to us through some person or some incident. But most often we have a clue of it as a child. I met a choreographer the other day. She choreographs for Bollywood movies. She has achieved remarkable success at a young age of twenty-one. I asked her, "When did you actually realize that this is what you want to do?" She said, "By the time I was ten-years-old, I had started coaching children. I had a natural flair for dance, and I knew that this is what I would want to do throughout my life. I go in a meditative state when I am performing. It transports me to a highly blissful level. Luckily, my parents supported and encouraged me and today I am a professional Choreographer."

All successful people invariably are passionate about what they do. It is said that Steve Jobs who was highly passionate about his work, looked for passion as a non-negotiable quality while hiring people for Apple. Influential leaders in all fields had this enduring quality in them. Their passion sharply focused on what they wanted to achieve and cut through all obstacles, oppositions, and negativity. Another interesting fact is that people with passion easily draw other people into their vision.

It is the passion that makes you stay up late and get up early in the morning. Passion helps relationships blossom. It breathes life into your years and fills it with power, energy, and meaning. And finally it makes you happy and blissful.

Reflections:
Passion is the key to success. And finding your passion and following it will certainly make you happy. The sooner you discover your passion and follow it, the happier you will be in life.

Step to Happiness:
Discover your passion and follow it. Find out what brings a sparkle to your eyes; what makes you forget all your problems and worries and most importantly, what makes your heart sing. There is always that inner voice talking to all of us, but we have learned a subtle art of silencing it. Once you dive within and listen to that voice you can find your passion.

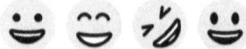

 *Happiness Mantra:*
Just for today, I do what I really love to do.

7

Key to Happiness is Healthy Relationships

Harvard study of 'Adult Development' that started in 1938 with Harvard sophomores, lasting for over 75 years, brought about startling revelations.

There were 724 participants in the study. The researchers studied the participants' health trajectories and their broader lives, including their success and failures in careers and marriage, and the findings truly astonished everybody including the researchers.

"The surprising finding is that our relationships and how happy we are in our relationships have a powerful influence on our health," said Robert Waldinger, director of the study, a psychiatrist at Massachusetts General Hospital and a professor of psychiatry at Harvard Medical School. "Taking care of your body is important, but tending to your relationships is a form of self-care too. That, I think, is the revelation."

The study revealed that close relationships keep people happy throughout their lives, more than money or fame. These bonds give them mental and physical strength, thus delaying the health decline. These ties are better predictors of long and happy lives than social class, IQ, or even genes.

Relationships are the most essential part of our existence. Living in isolation is difficult. Our emotional design is such that sharing our joys and sorrows alike with our near and dear ones, gives us a sense of comfort, and better strength to deal with the challenges in life.

When we achieve something, such as getting a promotion or buying a house we want to share it with the people around us, don't we? We feel happy when our accomplishments are acknowledged and appreciated. Similarly, when we are going through the low points in life, and can share it with people around, it helps us to better cope up with the lows and stresses. Building and nurturing relationships is a great investment one can make in life.

While writing this book, I did an interesting exercise. I spoke with about fifty children in the age group of 10 -15 years. I asked them one simple question, "What is it that you want the most in life when you grow up?" There were several answers such as earn money, fame, move places, become a pilot or a politician or an actor or a CEO of a company. But not even one kid said that 'I want to be happy' or "I want family and lot of friends."

In fact this is what happens with all of us. Ironically, whatever we want to achieve in life is with the aim of achieving happiness. It is implanted in our minds during our growing up years that getting a good job, buying a big car, buying a big house, getting married, and having children, will give us happiness. No one talks about building authentic relationships. In fact we take relationships for granted. We feel that our main aim in life is career, earning money and fame. But in the process, we miss out on nurturing the close relationships. There is an old person I know of. He is rich in terms of material wealth but does not have anybody around him. His whole life was focused on his career and earning money. He never had the time to develop relationships with his friends. His sons went abroad, and his wife passed away. He went into depression. He said, "I wish I had spent more time with my family and friends and developed good relationships." One needs to strike a balance.

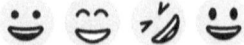

What stays with us till the end, are the people and the moments shared with them.

Today we live in the world subjugated by technology. Undoubtedly, technology has done wonders for our life. We have all the things required to lead a comfortable life. We can connect with anyone in any part of the world instantly, irrespective of where we are. We are exposed to an ocean of opportunities and possibilities, and all this has been possible only due to the technological revolution. The advent of smartphones and social media has tremendously increased the connectivity. You may feel closer to a person who is far away but you may be far from the person who is next to you.

We are mostly living in the virtual world – a world of 'click', 'like', 'comment' and 'share'. The whole new era of technology has also induced stress, anxiety, insecurity and depression in our lives. Research shows that depression, anxiety, and anti-social behaviour has phenomenally increased in the last decade. Loneliness is slowly becoming an epidemic. We are most of the times communicating with the machines and hardly talking to the people. A study says that an average person taps, clicks or swipes his smartphone 2617 times a day.

Here's some food for thought. How much time (forget the quality time) do we really spend with our loved ones. How many times do we strike a genuine, soulful conversation with them during the day? Television and smart phones have replaced even the good old dinner-time conversations.

Somewhere along the path, we have forgotten that we are

'emotional beings'. We often hold back our emotions as we don't have anyone to express them to. We have become so involved with our own lives, tending to our individual needs that we are hardly left with the time and energy to lend an ear to anyone else. We are also scared to be vulnerable and strive hard to maintain an illusory social image of a happy and confident person that we have created. We don't have a genuine someone to talk to, who would listen to us without taking advantage or being judgemental, love us the way we are, and protect our vulnerability. Heart-to-heart conversations have become rare. Most of our interactions with other people are superficial, with a formal, "Hi, How are you?" where we don't even wait for the other person to respond.

We are thus becoming an emotionally suffocated race, and these pent-up emotions manifest in the form of physical and mental illnesses. Many of us are therefore victims of loneliness and depression.

There was an interesting experiment carried out by Harry Frederick Harlow, an American Psychologist. For this experiment, he presented the infant rhesus macaques with a clothed mother and a wire mother under two conditions. In one situation, the wire mother held a bottle of food, and the cloth mother held no food. In the other case, the cloth mother held the bottle, and the wire mother had nothing.

Overwhelmingly, the infant macaques preferred spending their time clinging to the cloth mother. Even when only the wire mother could provide nourishment, the monkeys visited her just to feed. Harlow concluded that there was much more to the mother–infant relationship than milk and that this "contact comfort" was

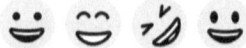

essential to the psychological development and health of infant monkeys and children.

Physical contact with an emotional comfort such as hugs releases hormones in the body that reduce the stress levels and make us happy.

As per the research carried out on the relation between friendship and happiness, friendship turns out to be the single most crucial factor in determining one's happiness. Even when we look back at life, the best and the happiest moments we have experienced in our lives are those with family and friends. Those memories naturally bring a smile to our face.

Studies have also proved that genuine friendships hold a lot of benefits. It not only makes life happier but also healthier and longer. Friends are our biggest strength and support. Don't we turn to them at the time of crisis or when we are stressed out? Just a simple conversation with them makes mountains look like molehills. It is a relationship of heart, and it only lets you be. Genuine, trustworthy, real friends are a blessing. Even if you have a few of them, you can consider yourselves amongst the wealthiest people on Earth.

There is an amazing, heart -touching story I came across and would like to share.

There was a war happening between the two countries. One soldier was severely wounded, and the other soldier who was his friend wanted to bring him back. His captain said, "There is no use going, your friend must be dead!"

However, the soldier still went ahead and brought his friend. Seeing the dead body, the captain said, "See, I told you. It was not worth it. Your friend is dead."

The soldier replied with moist eyes, "No Sir, it was really worth it. When I got to him, my friend saw me; he smiled and said his last words, "I knew you would come.""

How much ever we progress technologically, we will remain human beings with an emotional centre. We are always going to need someone to talk to, share our thoughts, be by our side, motivate us in our low times, support us emotionally, and give us strength mentally. Even the priciest of the material things in the world cannot fulfil any of these needs. We are going to need each other till eternity. So why not truly focus on building such relationships that are strong and soul-nourishing. I am confident that this will make our life's journey fulfilling, happy, and enjoyable.

Reflections:
Relationships are the very
core of our existence. In today's world when technology has
taken over our lives, we need to make an effort towards
nurturing authentic relationships. Healthy relationship keeps
us in the best of physical, mental and emotional health.

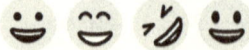

Step to Happiness:
Value the relationships you have. Nourish them with your time, care and love. Be there for your friends and family whenever they need you, even if it means going out of your normal course. Empathise with them and express your love and gratitude for them. This goes a long way in creating a strong bond.

Happiness Mantra:
Just for today, I take a baby step towards building healthy relationships.

8

The Art of
Now

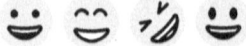

"Be happy for this moment.
This moment is your life."

- Omar Khayyam -

Here is one hilarious but thought-provoking Mulla Nasruddin story.

Mulla Nasruddin considered himself wise and boasted about his cleverness. One day in the court, the king said, "Mulla, You always brag about how clever you are. I will only agree that you are wise and clever if you can teach your donkey to read."

Nasruddin took the challenge thrown at him by the king and replied, "Of course your Majesty! That's quite an easy task."

"I will believe it only if you prove it," challenged the king.

"I mean it, and I can prove it to you," said Nasruddin.

The king said to Mulla in front of all the ministers in the court, "Are you ready to take it on as a challenge, then?"

"Yes, your Majesty," replied Nasruddin. "If you give me fifty thousand dollars right now, I promise that I will have taught my donkey to read by the end of the eight years."

The king agreed, but put a condition that if the donkey is not able to read by then, Mulla would be imprisoned and tortured every day. Both of them agreed to this deal, and Nasruddin left for home.

The next day, Nasruddin told his friend about what had happened at the king's court. His friend said, "Nasruddin, have you gone crazy? Teaching a donkey to read is next to impossible. Your donkey doesn't even stand still for a moment, and you say you are going to teach him to read in eight years. I think you are out of your senses. Be ready for the prison sentence friend."

"Relax my dear friend," replied Nasruddin calmly. "Eight years is a long time. There are three possibilities I can see happen. One, our king is old and may not be alive by then; second, even if he is alive, he may not be in power; and third, my friend, my donkey may not be alive by then!"

"What if none of these possibilities happen?" asked the friend.

"Well, if at the end of the seventh year if none of the above happens, I still have one year to think of a plan and escape the sentence," replied Mulla.

"Are you present here in the moment?" There is a possibility that while you are reading this, you may be thinking about the meeting with your boss this morning or your children's exam that is around the corner or about your promotion that is due or a vacation you are planning to take with your family or what to cook for dinner. At any given point in time, several thoughts are crossing our mind. Most often they are either about our past or about our future. However, the fact is that past has gone and future is yet to come.

The sure shot way to happiness is living in the present moment and experiencing it. The moment that you experience right now is the only moment that is real because past is history and future is a mystery.

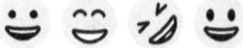

In the above story, the wise man Mulla Nasiruddin believes to live in the present moment and be happy. Though his friend highlights the possible outcome after eight years, Mulla Nasiruddin decides to cross the bridge when he reaches there. The fundamental reason for our unhappiness is worry. Worry, they say is like a rocking chair; it keeps you busy but does not take you anywhere. But sure enough, it steals the happiness out of the present.

Worry generally grows from a small seed planted in our mind, sometimes consciously and sometimes unconsciously. It is most of the times futile. Recently an incident happened to me when my brother gifted me the latest mobile phone, during his last visit to India. My happiness knew no bounds holding such a high-end phone in my hands. I had not even soaked myself thoroughly in this joy, when a thought crossed my mind, 'what if it slips from my hand and breaks...? And whoosh.......!!! My happiness flew out of the window. After that, I was more focused on 'what if it breaks' rather than the happiness of owning it.

As soon as our attention drifts away in the past or in the future, our happiness is replaced by fear, regret, guilt or worries and insecurities. Life is only in the present moment.

How can you remain in the present moment? By bringing the focus and attention in the now, and experiencing this moment with all your senses. Once you are able to do that, the only emotion you can experience is happiness. Vice-versa, if you ever feel a negative emotion, bring your attention back to the present moment.

Reflections:
Most often our mind wanders aimlessly in search of happiness forgetting that happiness lies in the present moment because the present moment is what life is!

Step to Happiness:
Be aware of every moment and be fully present in that moment. The best way to accomplish this is to focus on your breath. By doing this, you will be automatically pulled in the present moment even if your mind is wandering.

Happiness Mantra:
Just for today, I experience happiness here and now.

9

Follow your Dreams and Happiness will Follow you

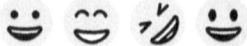

It was 25th October 2017 - one of the most memorable and happiest days of my life.

I was about 4360 miles away from my home in Mumbai, in a foreign land. I had set on an adventurous journey to Europe all by myself. Adventurous, because it was the first time, I ventured out of my home, alone, on an overseas trip. I was brought up in a small town in India in a highly protected and conservative environment where being a girl naturally entailed several boundaries. In our family, it was considered safe to have a male escort, when the females stepped out of the house. I lived a confined life for almost four decades. I was comfortable in the protected and secured space I was in; where fear, insecurity, anxiety existed on the periphery, and never really bothered me.

There is a famous quote, "A ship is always safe at the shore - but that is NOT what it is built for."

My husband motivated me to step out of the shore – my comfort zone, and explore the seas. I did plan the trip to Europe but often broke out into a cold sweat. Nevertheless, successfully handling all fears, anxieties, and insecurities, I boarded the flight to Paris – a dream destination for most people. Paris enchants you with its culture, food, fashion, and architecture. Being an Architect myself, it was my long-cherished dream to visit the Eiffel Tower- one of the architectural marvels of the world. I used to always wonder, how it would feel like to stand in front of this spectacular monument!

And there I was, in Paris, living my dream –standing in front of the

Eiffel Tower. I had to battle all odds to reach there. I knew nobody in town and language was a huge barrier. Since the time I landed there, my head was full of ifs and buts that were trying to instigate my already anxious mind. What if I am robbed? What if I lose my passport? What if I get lost? And all kinds of negative thoughts had already made their space in my head. But a strong wish to see the Eiffel Tower, gave me the strength to handle all fears. I figured out how to reach there, partly from the receptionist at the hotel who spoke broken English, and partly from the internet. I took a train to the Champ de Mars Metro station which is close to the Eiffel Tower and as I came out of the station and turned left, voila..! On my left, I got the first glimpse of the majestic structure, which humbly stood there since 1889. It was unbelievable. I soaked myself for a few moments in the exquisitely breath-taking, panoramic view before I started walking towards the Eiffel Tower.

I felt ecstatic. I felt a sense of accomplishment and contentment. I felt an indescribable peace within me. Such feelings are hard to put in words, they can only be felt. My anxiety, stress, insecurity simply disappeared, and only happiness prevailed in their place. It was an experience to cherish.

I am sure you must have experienced many such happy moments in your life too. It could be when you bought your first house, or you got your much deserved-promotion or when your child cleared a medical entrance exam or your daughter got married or when you visited your dream destination. All these events are usually preceded by stress, anxiety and worry, but as soon as you achieve the desired outcome, these emotions fade away, and

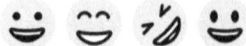

happiness peeps out from within. Fulfilling dreams or achieving goals induces a feel-good factor in us about ourselves and our lives. There is a sense of triumph, power, satisfaction, and well-being.

Dreams are something that makes our life going. They propel us to perform better in life and give meaning and direction to our survival. Life without dreams would be like a flower without fragrance.

I came across a wonderful poem by Langston Hughes, an African-American Poet.

Hold fast to dreams,

For if dreams die,

Life is a broken-winged bird

That cannot fly.

Hold fast to dreams,

For if dreams go,

Life is a barren field

Covered with snow.

So never ever stop dreaming. Following your dreams gives you an adrenaline rush, boosts your confidence, makes you feel good about yourself, provides a new direction to your life and above all makes you happy.

Reflections:
Dreams are the source
of energy. Never stop
dreaming. Dream about
what you want to achieve
and divert your energy in
achieving those goals.

Step to Happiness:
Make your dream list. It
includes anything that you
wish to achieve in life – big or
small. Resolve to pursue those,
one by one. Cross one when
done and move on to the next
one. By doing this you are sure
to live the most fulfilling life.

Happiness Mantra:
Just for today, I take one step towards my dreams.

10

Happiness Comes When Worry Goes

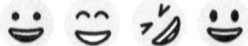

In a small village, there lived a farmer with his wife, son, and a horse. The farmer worked very hard all through his life and was getting old. One day his horse ran away. When the neighbours heard about this, they came to sympathize with him. "The only horse you had, ran away. Such bad luck," they said.

"Maybe," the farmer replied.

The next morning the horse returned, bringing with it three other wild horses. "Wow that's wonderful," the neighbors exclaimed.

"Maybe," replied the old man.

The following day, his son tried to ride one of the horses. However, since the horses were untamed, he fell and broke his leg. The neighbours came again and offered their sympathies over the misfortune that happened.

"Your only helping hand is now injured. Now you have to work single-handedly. That's sad." said the neighbours.

"Maybe," answered the farmer.

The very next day, some military officials came to the village to draft young men from the village in the army. When they saw that the farmer's son's leg was broken, they discounted him. This was like a blessing in disguise for the farmer.

The neighbours again turned up to congratulate the farmer on how well everything turned out to be.

"Maybe," said the farmer.

The farmer in the story was unperturbed by the good and bad that happened in his life. Generally, we are thrilled when something good happens and equally sad when something is amiss. We attach our happiness to the outcome of a situation and therefore cannot be in the state of bliss all the time.

We also tend to worry about the future when things don't seem to go the way we plan them. And, even if they are going as per our plan, we start worrying about 'what if they go wrong.' Either ways we end up always worrying. Moreover, worry is the biggest deterrent to happiness. Happiness and worry cannot exist together.

To stop worrying and start being happy we need to develop a higher perspective and more-in-depth understanding of life. Everything in our life is going perfectly as per the larger plan. Whatever is happening to us is for our highest good, even if it seems wrong on the surface. Life is full of surprises. At that time you may not understand what good comes out of a situation which looks unfortunate and ill-fated. What we need to do is stop worrying and start living, and when we start living, we are happy.

Situations in our lives are fluid. They keep on changing every moment. However, if we attach our happiness to the result, we can never be happy. Whatever problems or challenges we are facing today in any quadrant of our life, be it finance, relationship, career or health can miraculously change tomorrow. So when we are fretting about something that is transient, we are depriving

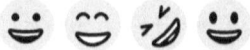

ourselves of the happy moments of today. Most often our worries are not of the present moment, but they are the projections of the future. Also, it may or may not be true.

There is a beautiful example of how we keep on worrying and why we shouldn't.

Charlie Chaplin once told a joke to the audience, and all the people started laughing.

He repeated the same joke, and only few people laughed.

He again repeated the same joke but this time no one laughed.

Then he said these beautiful lines,

"When you cannot laugh on the same joke again and again...then why do you cry again and again on the same worry."

So enjoy every moment of life and be happy...!

Life is beautiful!

Remember worry is something that we create out of our imagination; and if we have the ability to create something, we have the power to destroy it as well. So the next time you worry about something, you just need to wipe it off; and you will find happiness already existing there.

Reflections:
Worry is caused by our projection of things and situations that may or may not be true in the real sense. It starts in our head and spreads its roots throughout our entire being paralysing our happiness. Always thinking about it gives it the required fuel.

Step to Happiness:
Developing a higher understanding of life, faith, trust in our abilities and in those around us, will leave no place for worry. Self-talk works wonders. If you come across any situation that induces concern, observe your thoughts. If they are cascading in a negative spiral, ask yourself two simple questions, "Is the thing, situation or person I am worrying about under my control?" "Is my worrying going to bring in any positive change situation in the person?" If the answer is "No" then worrying is an absolute waste of your precious time and energy. One of the practices is to let go.

Happiness Mantra:
Just for today, I consciously choose to be self-aware and let go of the things I can't control.

11

Happiness is the Death of Ego

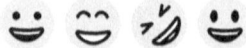

Once there lived a learned scientist who had many discoveries and patents to his credit. He was highly acknowledged in his field by his colleagues, and had also won several awards. He was working very hard, day and night, on a project that he thought would revolutionize the existence of humankind. After diligently working for years, he finally developed a formula using which he could reproduce himself. His work was so perfect and flawless that it was impossible to tell the reproduction from the original.

The scientist was very proud of himself that he could device such a formula. One day while doing his research, he realized that the Angel of Death was searching for him. He thought that it was the time to put his work to use. To stay immortal, he reproduced a dozen copies of himself to deceive the Angel of Death. The reproduction was so impeccable that they all looked the same. When the Angel of Death came down to fetch him, he was at a loss to understand which of the thirteen before him was the original scientist! He was utterly confused and not knowing what to do, left them, and returned back to heaven.

After a lot of deliberation in heaven and after consulting other Angels, the Angel of Death came up with a smart idea. He came back and addressing the thirteen scientists, said, "Sir, you are a genius. Your work is absolutely brilliant. I must congratulate you on making such a perfect reproduction formula of yourself. However, I have discovered a flaw in your work, just one tiny little flaw."

The scientist immediately jumped out and shouted, "Impossible! Where is the flaw?" "Right here," said the Angel, as he picked up the scientist from among the reproductions and carried him off. The whole purpose of the scientist and his formula of reproduction failed as he could not control his ego and lost his life.

While your Knowledge and Skills can take you to the top of the ladder and make you successful, the three-letter word "EGO" can pull you down immediately.

"You can be right or you can be happy," Gerald Jampolsky said.

When you are in an argument with somebody, what do you try to do? Do you genuinely try to prove your point or do you try to be right? If you do the latter means, you are operating from the clutches of your ego.

What is ego?

When someone is arrogant, thinks too high of himself, is selfish or self-centered, we say that the person has an ego or is an egotist.

Ego is nothing but a superficial structure around our true selves, which is our false identity. It comes from all the beliefs we have about our personality, talent, and abilities. Each one of us has an ego, and it forms a dynamic part of who we are. It is very difficult to see it, as it hides behind the image of ourselves that we have created and are convinced that, that is what we truly are. However, ego showcases itself in the emotional reactions we give such as, anger at loved ones, feeling of jealousy, need to control, need to be right, or impressing people around.

Although ego is associated with arrogance and feeling of superiority,

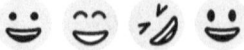

it also comes from low self-esteem and negative beliefs. This comes from projecting an image of security and confidence while struggling with feelings of insecurity, worthlessness, and inadequacy.

The mistake we often make is that we identify ourselves with our ego. But what we need remember is that ego is not us, but a separate part of us. Operating out of our ego often makes us unhappy.

Here are a few things that may help 'let go of the ego.'

Not taking everything personally: When we take things personally, we feel hurt or angry. We need to understand that when someone says something to us, that reaction is coming from his state of being. That person may be in a foul mood or acting out of his insecurities or may be deliberately trying to put us down. So it has to do nothing with us. So why should we take anything personally?

Need for Validation: Seeking appreciation or validation is the need of our ego. Since all of us are operating out of our egos most of the times, being judgmental about others comes naturally. Pleasing anybody is impossible. As soon as we drop the need for validation, we will be peaceful and happy.

Respond rather than react: In any communication, you either respond or react. A response comes from a peaceful state while reaction comes from a state of ego; it comes from a need to be right or need to control. Either of the two is harmful to relationships.

Don't get carried away by praises and labels: We as a society often plaster people with tags and approvals. We are in the habit of putting someone on a pedestal. This is fuel for our ego. It is important not to get carried away by it. What we need to remember is that 'we' are not this body, this profession, or not even the role we are playing in the family or society. We are beyond that. We are a part of the divine, and have come to this planet to experience human life. This understanding can be developed through the regular practice of meditation, and it prevents the bloating of the ego.

You must have seen some people who exude joy all the time while others move around as if they are carrying tons of weight. The joyous people don't have fewer challenges in life, it's only that they have learned to handle their ego well.

Reflections:
Ego is an extended part of us. However, that is not who we truly are. It is important to recognize our true nature and operate from that. Ego will only pave a path for our downfall and lead us to unhappiness. However, handling ego is the key to happiness.

Step to Happiness:
Replace ego with humility, love, kindness, and compassion.

Happiness Mantra:
Just for today, I choose to operate out of love, compassion, and empathy.

12

Be Curious, Not Judgemental

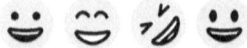

Once there was a 24-year-old boy travelling in a train with his father. As the train started, the boy looked out of the window and shouted, "Dad, look the trees are going behind!"

Then after a while, he again shouted with excitement, "Dad, look the clouds are running with us!" The boy looked thrilled and was beaming with happiness. He was so much into himself that he was oblivious of anybody in the train compartment. His father, who was sitting beside him, was smiling at him lovingly patting his back.

A young couple was sitting on the opposite seat. The couple was observing the behaviour of the young boy for a while. They were surprised by the childish behaviour of the boy. The young couple could not resist themselves and said to the old man, "Why don't you take your son to a good doctor?"

The old man smiled and said, "I did, and we are just going back home from the hospital. My son was blind since birth. He just got his eyes today."

The young couple was speechless, and they were ashamed of themselves for having said that.

We are often quick in judging someone without knowing anything about that person. As human beings, it comes very naturally to us. We have a specific set of logic that we have formed over the years, the conditioning of our mind and our beliefs that form the basis for judging others. Sometimes we are too fast in jumping to conclusions, without actually knowing the facts about the person or the situation. If we form an opinion about somebody based on these assumed facts, it may pose a considerable threat to developing good relationships, and generate negative emotions like anger, guilt, and jealousy. It could thus be one of the primary causes for unhappiness.

We look at the world from our perspective and expect people to behave in a certain way. When our expectations are not met, we pass a judgment about that person, based on our assumptions; "He is selfish" or "She is rude" or "He is short-tempered," and post that we look at that person in the same light. It is important to understand that the behaviour of a person at a given time is governed by a lot of factors. The person may not be in a good mood, may be going through some issues or may not be in the best of his physical health. However, these situations are temporary; so it may not be right to form an opinion about that person and retain it, based on the things that are transient. It is prudent not to judge people because every single person on this planet has a story and the truth sometimes might surprise you.

Human beings are bestowed with innate power and potential to be successful, and happy. However, most of us are not able to do so, you know why? Because we are judgmental about ourselves most of the times; telling ourselves "I am incapable of doing this" or "I am a loser" or "I am not as talented" and many more such statements. Forming judgment about oneself is nothing less than a self-sabotager. These judgments then turn into negative beliefs that prevent us from achieving our life goals. They, in turn, make us unhappy.

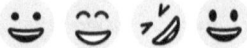

Judging others is an extension of self-judgment. Before embarking on the journey of personal growth and self-awareness, I was my own critic. Whatever I criticized in myself, I would see the same things in others. For example, my area of work was my anger. Moreover, everybody around me including myself said, "She gets angry on smallest of things," and I started believing that. So when I saw somebody getting angry, I easily formed a judgment "He/she is so short tempered." It almost became a habit to label, everyone, I came across. This habit put me on edge, snatching my happiness and peace from me.

When my awareness expanded and I worked on my stuff, I became more conscious and mindful of my thoughts. Each time I was tempted to label somebody, I would hear a voice within me saying, "Do you know the person fully?" If the answer was 'no' which often was, I told myself, "Then you have no right to judge that person." Nobody is perfect, neither am I. What we think about the other person is only 'our' perspective and perspective is only a viewpoint based on certain assumptions. It need not be the truth. The second question would be, "What would you do, react or behave if you were to be in that person's shoes?" and the answer would be, "probably the same way." This self-talk made me more empathetic towards that person and rather than getting angry or upset, I would think, how can I add value to this person's life, and the whole equation between the other and me would change radically.

The most important insight I have got on the path of self-discovery is that we all are on our individual soul journeys; therefore we should neither judge anybody nor compare ourselves with others. Following this will surely keep us happy.

Reflections:
We are quick at forming
an opinion without the full
know-how of the person or the
situation. Being judgemental
acts as a deterrent to building
good relationships and staying
happy in life.

Step to Happiness:
Whatever you think about
other person or the situation
is your perspective. It may
not always be true. Once you
understand this you will stop
being judgemental about
everything.

Happiness Mantra:
Just for today, I will accept people as they are
without being judgemental.

13

Acts of Kindness Bring Happiness

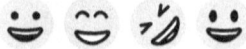

Once, two friends took off for a walk. They were so engrossed in chatting with each other that they did not realize when they reached the field. The Sun was shining over their heads, and so they thought of taking a break. They found shelter under a Banyan tree. As they sat under the tree, they noticed that there was a neatly folded stack of clothes and a pair of shoes carefully resting over a stone. As they looked around, they saw a man toiling in the farm.

The younger boy thought of a mischief and said to his friend, "Let's hide the clothes of this man behind the bush. When he comes to search for them, the expression he would have would be priceless."

The older boy looked at the clothes and said to the younger one, "The man seems to be poor. Look at his clothes. They are torn. I have an idea. We hide his shoes instead and put a silver coin in each shoe. When he discovers those, his expression will be priceless."

The younger fellow liked the idea. So they together hid the man's shoes in the bush behind and placed a silver coin in each one of them.

Since they wanted to capture the priceless expression of the man, they hid behind another bush.

After a while, the man came, changed his clothes and noticed that his shoes were in the bush. He removed those, and as he slid his feet in one shoe, he felt something between his toes. He bent and saw that it was a silver coin. He looked around and saw if someone had put the coin in his shoe. When he could not see anyone, he slid his second feet in the other shoe and again found a coin. He was pleasantly shocked to see another coin and could not believe his eyes.

The two boys were observing all this from behind the bush.

Thinking that he was alone, holding both the coins in his hands, the man started crying. They were the tears of relief and gratitude. Next, he knelt on his knees, and said a prayer in a loud voice. "Thank you God for this, and please bless the person who put the silver coins in my shoes! Now I can sell these coins and treat my wife who is in the hospital and feed my children who have not put even a morsel in their mouth since last evening."

Saying this he hurriedly got up and rushed towards his home.

After the man left, the two boys came out from their hiding and slowly walked back towards their home. They did not speak to each other as they were savoring the priceless expression they had just seen. They felt very happy for being kind to someone they did not even know. There was a smile on their faces and their soul danced with happiness.

"Kindness is a language which the deaf can hear, and the blind can see," said Mark Twain

There is a popular saying, "Bees live in hives, and humans live in tribes." We humans are designed to live in a community, and it is one of our prime responsibilities to help each other grow. Living together also calls for an important virtue, which is kindness.

Being kind to others has a boomerang effect. Research has shown that altruistic behavior releases endorphins in the brain and boosts happiness for us as well as the people we are kind to. Kindness

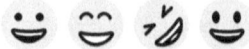

builds trust, and induces a sense of safety within the community. It increases the co-operation as every person who receives kindness likes to pass it on. Kindness is contagious. So, imagine if you are kind to a person, and that person is kind to another to another, how beautiful and happy place this world will be to live in!

Kindness is a primary trait of humans. We get many opportunities to be kind throughout the day. Just helping someone in need, without being selfish and judgmental is an act of kindness.

A small boy was walking along a beach. It was a low tide and numerous starfish had been washed up on the beach, were stranded and doomed to perish. The small boy picked each fish and took them back to water. A man was watching the boy do this. He went near the boy and said, "I can see you're very kind. But there must be thousands of them; it can't possibly make any difference."

Returning from the water's edge, the boy said, "It will for that one."

Simple things like offering your seat in the train to a person who needs it more than you, expressing gratitude to someone who helped you, doing something to make others happy, appreciating others for their good deeds, are very simple acts of kindness that you can do. These small things you do for others will not only make you and the other person happy but will also help create a bond between the two of you.

We are also bound by the 'law of karma'. It says that whatever you give comes back to you in manifolds. By being kind to others, we only invite positive things in our life. Being kind to others is an instant solution to feel good about ourselves, be happy and spread happiness.

Reflections:
Kindness is one of the most fundamental virtues every human should practice. This includes Kindness towards every living being. It has a rebounding effect. Being kind attracts love, prosperity and good health in our life.

Step to Happiness:
Be the kindest person you ever know. One of the many regrets that we have on our deathbed is that 'I was not kind enough'. Consciously practice at least one act of kindness every day and integrate it into your life.

 *Happiness Mantra:*
Just for today, I will be the kindest person ever.

14

Letting Go of Anger

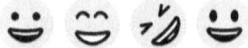

Long ago there lived a monk. He lived in a monastery that was close to a serene lake surrounded by lush green trees. He followed all the religious practices regularly and progressed on the spiritual path. However there was one thing that was pulling him back, and that was his anger.

One day he thought of meditating in solitude, away from his monastery.

He rowed his boat out to the middle of the lake, secured it there, closed his eyes and began to meditate.

After a few hours of undisturbed silence and bliss, he suddenly felt the bump of another boat colliding with his own. Slowly he sensed his anger rising, he was disturbed and lost focus. Who was this boatman who dared to disturb his meditation? When he could not control his rising temper any longer, he opened his eyes, and as he was about to scream at the boatman for disturbing his meditative state, he saw that the boat was empty that may have probably got untethered and floated to the middle of the lake.

It was a moment of epiphany for the monk. At that moment, the monk achieved self-realization, and understood that the anger was within him; and it merely needed the bump of an external object to provoke it out of him.

From then on, whenever he came across someone who irritated him or provoked him to anger, he reminded himself, "The other person is merely an empty boat. The anger is within me......"

In reality, we all have the anger within us, all the time,

All it needs is someone, like the empty boat, to provoke it

When I was young, I often used to be irritable and grumpy. I was not able to decipher the emotion that I was experiencing, but I remember being labelled as a short-tempered person, who would get angry at the drop of the hat. What made me angry? Anything and anyone. I started identifying with that 'angry' me and accepted that I am an angry person. It made things easy for me. Because when people said you are short-tempered, I would say, "Yes I know I am short-tempered." However, I did not entirely agree with it. Deep inside I knew that I was a loving, kind and peaceful person. There was always a conflict within which made me miserable most of the times. I did not experience true happiness. My being was clouded by the identity thrust upon me as I grew up.

As I stepped on the spiritual path, in search of my true self and other questions about life, there were a lot of revelations. I got three realizations a) The anger is not me, but it is one of the emotions I experience b) Anger is only a reaction to some deeper emotional turbulence, and c) The understanding that it is okay to be angry and vent out the anger without hurting anybody. This understanding brought in acceptance and drove away the resistance and the conflict. I could identify the triggers that evoked the anger in me and learned to handle them. Over time, love that was a stronger emotion took over, and there was only peace and happiness after that.

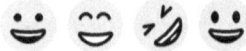

When a person is angry, he is very likely to take wrong decisions, say things that shouldn't be said and repent later. He can indulge in guilt and burn himself out completely.

Anger is a powerful emotion. It can spoil relationships, it can break business deals, it can wear you down, it can lead to physical, emotional and mental disorders; in short, it can make you completely unhappy.

The trigger of anger can be different in different people, and the triggers are always going to be there. The art lies in how you stay unaffected by any provocations by dealing with them and let go of the anger quickly if you ever get angry.

Here are a few tips:

- 20 minutes of brisk walk or any other physical activity reduces stress and thus preventing the anger from setting in.

- Remind yourself that anger doesn't fix anything, it only makes matter worse. Think calmly about handling the situation.

- The best way to blow off anger is to add humour to the situation. Look at it through funny eyes, or watch a comedy show or read a joke.

- Forgiveness is a marvellous tool to let go off the anger. Forgive the person who has angered you, not for him but yourself. It not only reduces your anger but also sets you free.

- Relaxation is the key. Even in the most challenging situations, the more you relax, the less agitated you feel,

- Practice some form of meditation and breathing exercise.

Reflections:
The higher understanding that anger is just a passing emotion triggered by something that happens outside of us gives us an opportunity to look at it objectively. If we are able to do that, we realize that anger is futile.

Step to Happiness:
Whenever any situation arises that makes you angry, go inward and look what has triggered it, instead of reacting. Get into a habit of minimum 10 minutes of reflection, introspection, and meditation every day.

 *Happiness Mantra:*
Just for today, I will get in touch with my deeper self that is full of love and divinity.

15

Be You – it's a Lot Easier Than Faking it

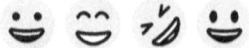

There is an exciting fable I came across.

Once there lived an emperor in the Far East. He was honest and was loved and respected by everyone in his kingdom. As he was growing old, he thought that the time had come to select a new successor. He thought of an idea. Instead of a regular practice of choosing one of his assistants or his children, he decided to do something different. He called a gathering of all the young people, and addressed them, "I am old now, and I feel that this kingdom now needs a young emperor. And this time, I have decided to choose one amongst you."

This unexpected announcement shocked one and all. The emperor continued, "I have found a way of selecting one of you as the next Emperor. Today I am going to give seed to each one of you. It is a very special seed. What you have to do is plant that seed, water it, nurture it and come here with a plant exactly after one year. Based on the plants you bring, I will judge and choose the next emperor."

In the crowd, there was a young and an innocent boy named Ling. Like others he also got a seed. He was very excited and went home and told his mother the entire story. She helped him get a pot and soil, and he planted the seed. Ling watered it every day with much love and care. Every morning, he would go near the pot to see if the seed had sprouted, and water it. He took great care of his pot and kept it away from pests and animals.

After about three weeks of the planting of seed, when he met his other friends; they started talking about how beautifully the plants had begun to grow. Ling kept checking everyday, but his seed did not show any sign of sprouting.

Weeks passed by, and Ling's friends had plants that also started flowering, but with Ling's seed, there was no sign of any life. Six months passed by, but Ling's seed had no plant, while others were happily talking about their grown-up plants.

Ling was sure that he had killed the seed. He felt like a big failure. But he gathered hope and kept on watering the seed thinking that one day a plant might just come out.

When everyone else started discussing how well all of their plants were growing, Ling was quiet. He just kept waiting and waiting.

Finally, one year passed by and on a day decided, all the youth brought their plants to the emperor for inspection. Ling told his mother that he would not take the empty pot to the emperor. But his mother insisted and said that it is always good, to be honest about what happened. He knew that his mother was right and took the empty pot to the palace. When Ling arrived at the palace, he was amazed to see the variety and the huge plants grown by other youth. They were the most beautiful plants he had ever seen. He put his empty pot beside them. His friends and other youth made fun and laughed at him. A few also felt sorry for him and consoled him saying, "Hard luck Ling, but good try nevertheless."

When the emperor entered the room, Ling tried to hide at the back so that he could save himself from the shame in front of the emperor. When he saw all the plants, the emperor said, "My, what great plants, trees, and flowers you have grown. Today is the day

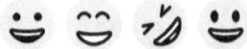

when one of you will be appointed as the next emperor!" Suddenly the emperor spotted Ling hiding at the back with his plant-less pot. He ordered his guards to get Ling in front of him. Ling was terrified. He was sure that the emperor would have him killed because of his failure to grow the plant.

When he came in front, the emperor asked him his name. "My name is Ling." He replied, scared to death. Everyone present there started laughing. The emperor signalled everyone to be quiet. He looked at Ling, and then announced to the crowd, "Behold your new emperor! His name is Ling!"

Everyone present there was stunned. How could Ling become their new emperor? He could not even grow a seed. Looking at the confused faces of the youth there, the emperor said, "I gave a seed to each one of you one year ago. I had instructed you to plant the seed, water it, and bring it back to me today. However, there was a catch. I gave you all boiled seeds which would not grow. All of you, except Ling, have brought me trees and plants and flowers. Probably when you found that the seed would not grow, you substituted another seed for the one I gave you. It was only this young lad who had courage and honesty to bring me a pot with my seed in it. Therefore, he is the one who will be the new emperor!"

It is not only a lot easier to be what you are, and truthful about it, but is also equally rewarding.

Being honest brings inner peace. You are relieved from the burden of faking anything.

If you speak one lie, you have to speak thousand lies to justify that one lie. This demands you to be alert all the time and induces a lot of stress. It makes you anxious and uprooted. Whereas if you are honest, there is no conflict, and you are in perfect harmony with yourselves and happiness flourishes in your being.

We generally try to be pretentious due to the fear of rejection. It's a human need to be accepted and acknowledged. We try to fit into an image that another person has about us. This compulsion to fit in the frame perceived by others takes us away from our real authentic selves, which is our true identity. If we start behaving this way we soon lose touch with our core and pave a path to unhappiness.

We need to understand that none of us is perfect. Each one of us is unique. So let us acknowledge it and live that way. Loving and accepting ourselves the way we are does not leave any space for pretension.

When you are in sync with what we think, say and do, you come across as an honest and genuine person, and everybody wants to be in the company of such people. Most importantly it will make you happy.

Reflections:
'Honesty is the best policy', they say, and it is true. Being honest to yourself or being who you are is a lot easier than making up and faking things. It makes you peaceful and calm from within and does not leave any space for stress.

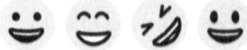

Step to Happiness:
Never try to impress someone.
Because by doing that, you
try to fit into their image of
you. This can make you live a
hollow life. To stay happy, be
who you are.

Happiness
Mantra:
Just for today, I
will get in touch
with my deeper
self that is full of
love and divinity.

16

Miracles Do Happen

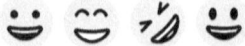

Sifa was the only daughter who lived with her parents in one of the suburbs in Mumbai. She belonged to a family that had orthodox views. The females in their family did not have the privilege of education. Their prime responsibility was taking care of the house and the rearing of children. However, Sifa's parents were liberal in their views and gave her all the freedom that a boy in the family enjoyed. They were determined to provide her with a good education, as they were deprived of the same.

Sifa's father worked in a factory and mother was a homemaker. She managed the house efficiently in the meagre salary earned by her husband.

When Sifa was in the 10th grade, an unfortunate incident occurred. There was an indefinite strike in her father's factory, and as a result, he did not get salary for many months. They had to take a loan from friends and relatives to manage their living. Their financial situation went from bad to worse. There was no sign of an end to the strike and Sifa's parents were immersed in debts. A time came when Sifa's school fees had to be paid without which she could not appear for the board exams. They had already exhausted all their resources, and more funds could not be arranged from anywhere. Her parents were distraught. Sifa could not bear to see the condition of her parents and decided to quit her studies. Though the decision was tough for them, they practically had no choice. With a heavy heart, they accepted the situation and surrendered to the Almighty.

Little did they know then, that a miracle was to happen the next day.

Next morning, when Sifa and her parents were engaged in a serious discussion, agonised over the problem, they heard a knock on the door. Sifa's mother opened the door and was shocked to see her cousin brother, who was a lawyer, standing there was holding a briefcase. She had broken ties with her side of the family as her father-in-law wanted it that way. Seeing him at the door, she was amazed. They had lost touch long ago, and he didn't even know her whereabouts. Hesitantly, she invited him into the house. After exchanging pleasantries, she asked him the purpose of his visit. He told her that he had a tough time locating her as he did not have her contacts. He then took out a cheque from his briefcase and handed it over to her saying that it was a part of her share of the inherited property that she was entitled to.

This was no less than a miracle. The amount they received not only took care of Sifa's school fees but also paid their debts with enough surplus to manage their expenses for a few months.

Miracles do happen.

We are a part of the whole consciousness at play. Everything that happens in our life, and every person we meet, has a significant role to play in shaping up our life. Every incident is beautifully orchestrated, occurring perfectly, at the right time and as per the larger plan. Because we fail to see this, we get dejected when things turn out as planned by us. However, if we could only trust the process of life and go with the flow, we would be able to see life with an awe.

Isn't it a miracle that all the organs of our body are working in perfect unison, to keep us moving? Isn't it a miracle that the oxygen we breathe purifies the whole blood in our body within a fraction of a second and our heart keeps on supplying blood to various organs to keep us alive? Isn't it a miracle that we can feel, think and co-create?

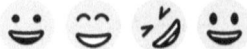

If you look at life from that 'innocent you,' you will experience a miracle at every step in your life. Your attention will go to the beautiful nature God has created, thousands of floras and faunas, beautiful terrains, awesome hues of oranges, yellows and blues carpeting the sky – all this is nothing short of a miracle. The unbelievable technological inventions made by man, the mind-blowing architecture that man has created, the luxuries that we experience, are all miracles.

We just need to change our perspective and we will see a miracle in everything. This will certainly make us happy in life. We just need to trust the process and believe in power of miracles.

Reflections:
At times we get too depressed by failures or things not going our way. But if we can change our perspective of seeing things, look at everything with awe, and acknowledge the unfaltering way in which the entire universe operates, we will only be happy in our lives.

Step to Happiness:
Whenever any situation pulls you down, believe that it is transient and just a small part of the bigger show. Trust that miracles do happen.

 *Happiness Mantra:*
Just for today, I trust the process of life.

17

Practicing Detachment From Material Things

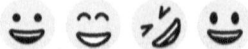

Once there was a boy who was born to a wealthy merchant. As he grew up, his father thought that it would be an excellent idea to show him how poor people live, so that he knows the importance of all the riches that he has and understands how happy he is in life.

So they went to the countryside, to the farm of a poor family that the father had figured out. They spent several days there. On their return, the father, "So, how was the trip son?"

"Oh, it was wonderful, dad" – the boy replied.

"Did you notice how poor people live and how fortunate you are?"

"Yeah, I did," said the boy. The father was eager to hear his son's views on the trip they had.

"Well dad, I noticed a few things - we have only one dog, and they have four o. In our garden, we have a swimming pool, while they have a river that has no end. We've got imported chandeliers, but they have stars above their heads at night. We have the patio, and they have the whole horizon. We have only a small piece of land, while they have the endless fields. We buy food, but they grow it. We have a high fence for protection of our property, and they don't need it, as their friends protect them."

The father was flabbergasted with his son's reply. He didn't know what to say.

Then the boy added, "Thank you, dad, for letting me see how happy those people were."

'I will be happy when my husband buys me a diamond set,' 'I will be happy when I own a house,' 'I will be happy when I have a Mercedes,' 'I will be happy when I have a lot of money.' Do you often catch yourself thinking about the above things? And do you link your happiness to those? If yes, then there is a great possibility that you are not happy. What you are doing is probably procrastinating your joy.

When we link our happiness to something outside us, we can always find excuses not be happy. Material things can never give us lasting happiness. If you buy a Mercedes, you will look for a Rolls Royce. If you have a diamond ring, you would want a necklace. If you have a 1000 square feet house you may wish to have a 2000 square feet one.

The desire to want more is endless. However, 'desire' per say is not wrong; as it gives you the energy to achieve your goals and a drive to perform and reach your highest potential. What is terrible is letting your happiness be dependent on those achievements and possessions.

There was a wealthy man who had a high-end car, and he loved it to no bounds. So much so that he would not let anybody touch it and used to clean it himself. One such morning as he stepped into the garage, he noticed that his son had a sharp object in his hand and was scribbling something on the car. The rich man got so angry that he picked up an iron rod lying nearby and hit the boy on his leg with such force that his leg started bleeding. Soon realizing his mistake, the man took his son to the hospital. However, the damage was already caused. The boy became crippled. While the boy was still in the hospital, when the man came home, he went near his car which was wholly cladded with dust. He took a cloth and wiped the area where his son was fidgeting

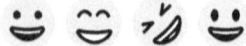

with the car. What he saw made him drown in the seas of guilt forever. The boy had scribbled, "I love you dad" on the car. The man could not forgive himself for what he had done to his son.

When we are attached to our material possessions, we often get so over-powered by them that we fail to look at the blessings in our lives. And this often leads to unhappiness.

Material things do not measure true wealth and happiness; however, it is measured by love, genuine relationships, and freedom.

Reflections:
We are born on this earth to experience everything around us. Desiring and aiming for material wealth is not bad. Material things give us ease and comfort in life. But attaching our happiness to those things can lead to misery.

Step to Happiness:
Practicing detached attachment will undoubtedly open the door to happiness. It can be achieved through the continued practice of meditation where you understand your true self and the ephemeral quality of life.

 *Happiness Mantra:*
Just for today, I will focus on love and relationships and value them more than material things.

18

Happiness is Peace of Mind

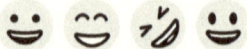

Once, Buddha was travelling with some of his followers through the forest. As they went ahead, they passed by a lake. Pointing at the lake, Buddha said to one of his followers, "I am thirsty. Please go and get some water from that lake for me."

As the follower reached the lake, a bullock cart started passing through the water, due to which the water became muddy and unclean.

The disciple thought that he could not give that water to his Guru to drink.

So he returned to Buddha and told him, "The water in the lake is unclean, and so I could not get it for you."

After about half an hour, Buddha asked the same disciple to go back and fetch some water from the lake.

The disciple went back and found that the water was still the same.

He came back and informed Buddha about it.

After sometime, again Buddha asked the same disciple to go back.

This time, when the disciple went, he found that the mud had settled down, and the water was clear.

So he collected some water in a pot and brought it to Buddha.

Buddha looked at the water, and then he looked up at the disciple and said,

"Now tell me what did you do to make the water clean?"

Looking at the confused face of the disciple, Buddha continued, "What you did was you let the water be, and the mud settled down on its own. Now you have the clean water. Your mind is exactly like that. When it is disturbed, just let it be. Give it a little time. It will settle down on its own. You don't have to put in an effort to calm it down. It will happen. It is effortless."

The fundamental nature of our soul is peace. However, it gets polluted by our response to the challenges and situations that life poses in front of us.

We think that peace is all about doing something, that getting peace is a strenuous job, and so on. On the contrary, peace is precisely the opposite. It is an effortless process. Peace is just in the being and not doing.

Life will always pose a threat to our happy and peaceful state of mind through various challenges and situations leading to agitation, frustration, irritation, sadness, anxiety, and depression. We are emotional beings, and we are bound to experience all these emotions. However, how many times do we give these emotions a chance to settle down? When we are agitated or irritated, we react, and the reaction further creates a whirlpool of negative emotions. However, like in the Buddha story above, what if we give these emotions a chance to settle down? As soon as we detach ourselves from them and leave them for a while, we can regain our peace.

We often feel that the people and situations around us disturb our

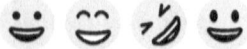

peace. I have heard people saying that when they are with nature, they feel peaceful and as soon as they are back to the city their peace disappears. Sure enough, the peace that they feel is that of nature.

This brings us to an essential point that peace is an innate character of our being. However, we give power to the situations, circumstances, and people around us to disturb our peace. So how does that happen?

A few days back we were participating in a book fair. It was a hugely successful day from a business point of view, and I was particularly happy as I met some wonderful people there and signed copies of my first book 'Wake Up' for the readers. An ex-colleague who had switched jobs also visited our booth. I greeted her with a warm hug and was happy to see her. She looked a bit estranged and during our conversation asked me, "So, how's your publishing house doing?" "Very well!" I said, "From two titles a month we have moved on to doing around eight to ten and that too the best ones." She looked surprised. "But people really don't know you in the market, and many times I advise people to buy books from you."

Our conversation was interrupted by someone from my office who wanted to talk to me. The day passed by with more book signing and interacting with new people. However, as I was driving back home, I was feeling irritated and had lost my sense of peace, in spite of the day being successful. I reviewed the entire sequence of events that took place during the day, and I realized that it was the conversation that took place with my ex-colleague that disrupted my peace. As soon as

I realized the cause, I pondered upon it and thought to myself, "The conversation was not at all worth giving my focus, attention and time." With this awareness, my irritation was replaced by sympathy for her, and I regained my lost peace and happiness.

On many occasions, our peace is lost because of the conflict created between our thoughts, speech, and action. For example, I think I should not be doing business with Mr. X as because we don't share the same values, but I get into sweet talking with him and end up doing business. It gives rise to a massive conflict within me as what I think/feel, say and do is not in sync with each other. The result being I will be unhappy.

Once a distressed person went to a wise man and said, "I want peace. What do I do?"

The wise man replied, "It is simple. Remove 'I,' that's ego. Remove 'want,' that's desire...and 'peace' is all yours."

We all seek that which is our inherent nature, outside of us. Sometimes when we are working towards achieving our goals, we get too stressed about achieving the goal and lose our peace over it and forget that even the journey towards that goal needs to be experienced.

You must have experienced that a peaceful person spreads peace around him and an agitated person will spread agitation. After all, you can only give what you have.

Whenever we lose our peaceful state of mind due to whatever

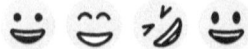

reason it may be, it changes our breathing pattern. One of the easiest, fastest and surest ways to regain peace is by catching the breath. When we experience a conflict arising within, our breathing automatically becomes rapid and shallow. This sets the tone for a spiral of negative emotions. This process can be reversed by stabilizing the breath again. This can be done by being conscious about each breath and observing it. Being with your breath turns the negative emotional spiral into a positive one, and you feel happy and peaceful again.

Reflections:
By default, the nature of our being is peace. This peaceful state is affected by various external factors on a day to day basis. One needs to be conscious of the thought process and when and how it changes its tone. Once that is established, it is not difficult to regain the peaceful state.

Step to Happiness:
Practice being in a peaceful state, by being with your breath for minimum five minutes every day. This will train your mind to experience innate peace and will help you to change your mind from an agitated to a peaceful state.

Happiness Mantra:
Just for today, I experience the internal peace throughout my entire being.

19

Gratitude is the Sure shot Way to Happiness

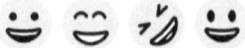

There came a point when my life was in shambles. My father-in-law was critically ill and was in and out of the hospital. My mother-in-law, who was in an advanced state of Alzheimer's, suffered a stroke and her left side got paralysed. All our resources and time got diverted to the two old patients in our family of four. Since both of us were working independently, our work came to a standstill. Slowly all our savings depleted as the hospital bills piled up. We had to hire caretakers to look after them and a person to take care of the household tasks. Hiring help gave us the freedom to work and move around. We had heard many discouraging stories, about the caretakers. However, fortunately, we had a staff of three who was dedicated, loyal and committed. So the new phase of our life began where we needed to make changes to our routine and lifestyle.

When we go through trying times in our lives, we generally tend to focus on the lack and what is not right. Same happened with me too. Since I was amidst the chaotic life, I could not see the situation it in perspective. Once, my friend visited us to meet my in-laws. She herself had also gone through a tough task of single-handedly taking care of her ailing mother, who had passed away a few months backs. When I was sharing my story with her, she said, "Aruna, you guys are truly blessed. You have such a fantastic support staff that allows you the freedom to work and carry on with your lives. When my mother was sick, I had a major challenge in this area. In spite of paying a hefty amount, the caretaker would not turn up without informing and my schedule for the entire day would go haywire. It badly affected my personal and professional life."

When she said this, it dawned upon me how blessed I am. I just needed to change my perspective of looking at things. After that, I started valuing people around me more than before. I would not leave a single opportunity of thanking them and appreciating them for the work they did....and the result? I started getting more support from them than before. They would often go out of their way and help me out with other jobs as well. Looking at the situation through grateful eyes made me and people around me happier and eased out the rough patch that we were going through.

Such is the power of gratitude. When you are grateful about every small thing in life, your life is sure to take a magical turn, beyond your expectations.

If someone tells you to be grateful when you are wading through the rough waters of your life, it may seem like a bad joke! However, in the worst of situations, this is the only way you can turn the tables around.

Two psychologists, Dr. Robert A. Emmons of the University of California, Davis, and Dr. Michael E. McCullough of the University of Miami, have done much research on gratitude. In one study, they asked all participants to write a few sentences each week, focusing on particular topics.

One group wrote about things they were grateful for that had occurred during the week. A second group wrote about daily irritations or things that had displeased them, and the third wrote about events that had affected them (with no emphasis on them being positive or negative). After ten weeks, those who wrote about gratitude were more optimistic and felt better about their

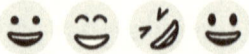

lives. Surprisingly, they also exercised more and had fewer visits to physicians than those who focused on sources of aggravation.

Expressing gratitude works magically in every area of life. If you show gratitude towards your partner, your relationship is sure to flourish, or if you say 'Thank you' to your colleagues or your assistants, they are sure to feel motivated to do more work, if you express gratitude to your friends, your friendship will surely grow thicker.

My husband and I had conducted a workshop for children on how to achieve excellence in life. One session in the workshop was on gratitude. We asked the children, "Do you ever say 'Thank you' to your parents for whatever they do for you?" Out of thirty children only two raised their hands. One child Richa asked, "But why do we need to thank them. They love to do things for us." During the creative session in the workshop Richa had mentioned about making a birthday card for her mom. So I asked her, "Richa, what did your say do when you gave her the birthday card you so lovingly and painstakingly made?" Richa said, "She kissed and hugged me and thanked me and said that it was the best card she had ever received." Richa got her answer in her reply only. Next day, Richa's mom called me and said, "I don't know what you taught these children!" She was in tears. "After the workshop, my daughter came home and thanked me for every small thing. She was so appreciative of the dinner I cooked, she helped me clear the table, she said thanks for being my mom, you are the best mom in the world...!" Richa's mom was so touched and overwhelmed that she could not speak any further.

Expressing gratitude for everything makes life so much better.

Studies have shown that adopting an attitude of gratitude works wonders in every area of your life. It keeps you healthy, improves your relationships, helps you lead a better social life, boosts your self-esteem and helps you move faster towards your goal. So making gratitude a way of life works enormously well.

Acknowledge and appreciate people around you. Even if you are not able to do it physically, the act of thanking a person mentally works equally well. It releases the feel-good hormones in your bloodstream and makes you a happier person. It changes your attitude towards the situation or the person, and this creates a positive energy field around yourself.

The surest way to come out of any depressing, stressful or negative situation is by counting your blessings.

Reflections:
An attitude of gratitude is the way of life. Though it is difficult to be grateful in the worst of the situations, it's only gratitude that has the power to pull you out of any such situation.

Step to Happiness:
If you want to change your state of mind instantly....be grateful. It helps to start and end your day with a gratitude prayer. Fall into the habit of counting your blessings, and you will always feel, happy, energetic and positive.

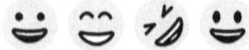

> **Happiness Mantra:**
> *Just for today, I am grateful to God for giving me such a wonderful life, for the people around me, for the food I eat, for the air I breathe, for the water I drink, for the house I live in, for the perfect body I have. (You can add more to the list)*

20

Contentment Brings Happiness

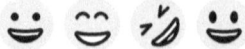

"Contentment is natural wealth;
luxury is artificial poverty."

- Socrates -

Here's another interesting story of Mulla Nasruddin. One day, Mulla Nasruddin went to meet his neighbour. The neighbour seemed to be miserable and in pain. Mulla asked him, "You look miserable. What is bothering you?"

The man said, "I have such a small house. We are six of us - my wife and I, our three children and my sick mother-in-law - we all live in such a small and stuffy space. There's not even enough space to move around. Mulla, can you help me find a solution to this grave issue that I am facing?"

Nasruddin said, "How many chickens do you have in your backyard?"

"Ten of them," said the neighbour.

"Good. So bring them inside the house and keep them there," said Nasruddin.

"But, Mulla!" the man exclaimed. "My house is already overcrowded."

"Just do as I say," Nasruddin replied.

The man was desperate and wanted a quick solution to his problem, so he followed Mulla's advice. He went and got all the chickens inside his little cottage.

Next day, he went to meet Mulla again and said, "Mulla, I did exactly as you said, and got the chickens into the house. But it did not solve my problem. In fact, it has worsened. My house is even more stuffed now.

"I see," said Nasruddin pretending to think. "You've a donkey, right? Get him inside your house." The man thought Mulla must be crazy. How could he fit the donkey in an already crowded house? But somehow Nasruddin managed to convince him that by doing that he was moving one step closer to the solution to his problem.

The following day, the man came to Mulla, looking distressed, and said, "Mulla, we hardly have any space to move inside the house. The total count now is six of us, ten chickens, and a donkey inside my house."

Nasruddin replied, "You own a goat too, don't you?"

"Yes, I do," said the man.

"Great," Nasruddin said. "Take it inside the house too."

Now the man got mad at Mulla Nasruddin, "Have you gone insane? Are you helping me or making my life hell? How is that going to solve anything?"

But Mulla Nasruddin remained calm and said, "This is the last thing you need to do, and all your problems will be sorted. Trust me." Since the man was desperate and was halfway through into Mulla's advice, he decided to listen to him one last time.

The next day, the man went to meet Mulla Nasruddin. He was furious

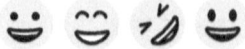

and shouted, "Your plan is no good. It has made our lives completely miserable. The house is so crammed now that it is even impossible to breathe. My family is mad at me for listening to your stupid advice."

"Don't get so upset, friend," said Mulla. "The solution to your problem is right in front of your eyes. Go home and remove all the animals and put them outside your house." The man had no option but to listen to Mulla in this dire situation.

Next day, the man came to Nasruddin, beaming with happiness. He said, "I can't thank you enough, Mulla! You are a genius. Your plan worked so well. After putting all the animals outside, there is enough space in the house for all my family. Everyone is now happy and content with the house."

We live in a world of artificial poverty where everyone is running after something or the other not really knowing where; and inviting dissatisfaction and unhappiness into our lives, in the bargain.

What is contentment? A quick trip to the dictionary defines contentment as a state of happiness and satisfaction. Being content does not mean that you do not have any goals in life and you stop growing and evolving. That is complacency. Contentment is a beautiful space where you feel happy and satisfied with what you have and where you are, and you want to move towards the betterment of that state.

If I am a content person, I might want to try out that new phone in the market because it has additional features and it renders a richer user experience. If I am a discontent person, I may want the new phone because my friend has it or I want to show off, or I want to put someone down.

Once, there lived a farmer named Hafiz, in Africa who was happy and content. One day a wise man came and told him about the glory of diamonds and the power that comes with it. He said, "If you had a diamond of the size of your thumb, you could own a city. If you had a diamond the size of your fist, you could probably own your own country." And then he went away.

That night the farmer couldn't sleep. His state of mind changed to that of unhappiness and discontentment. The next morning he woke up with the intention of selling his farm and made arrangements, took care of his family and left his village in search of diamonds.

Hafiz wondered all over Africa but couldn't find any. He went through all of Europe and couldn't find the diamonds. While he was still hunting for the treasure, he was emotionally, physically and financially broke. He got so disheartened that he threw himself into a river and committed suicide.

Back home, the person who had bought his farm was watering the camels at a stream that ran through the farm.

Across the stream, the rays of the morning sun hit a stone and made it sparkle like a rainbow. He thought it would look good on the mantelpiece. He picked up the stone and put it in the living room. That afternoon the wise man came and saw the stone sparkling. He asked, "Is Hafiz back?" The new owner said, "No, why do you ask?" The wise man said, "Because that is a diamond. I recognize one when I see it."

The man said, "No, that's just a stone I picked up from the stream. Come, I'll show you. There are many more." They went and

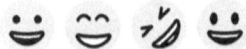

picked up some samples and sent them for analysis. Sure enough, the stones were diamonds. They found that the farm was indeed covered with acres and acres of diamonds.

We all are like the farmer. We are wandering everywhere in search of happiness and contentment but don't realize that these two exist together right here right now. It's just a matter of acknowledging their presence. Happiness does not depend on what you have or what you do. It is present within you. You just need to realize it.

Reflections:
Contentment does not depend on what or how much you have but depends on how you feel about what or how much you have. Contentment and happiness go hand in hand.

Step to Happiness:
Having an attitude of gratitude, helping others, not comparing, accepting challenges and difficulties with grace and moving towards the betterment of self will take you to the content zone of your life.

Happiness Mantra:
Just for today, I am happy and contended here and now.

21

Understanding Life

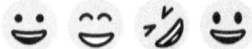

Akbar was coroneted at an early age and built on one of the greatest empires of his times. He lived a life of extravagance. He was surrounded by people and courtiers who always flattered him and agreed to whatever he said. Perhaps, this made Akbar arrogant, and he behaved as if he controlled the whole world.

One day, Birbal decided to make Akbar realize this nature of his and teach him a lesson on life.

One evening as Akbar was going towards his palace through the garden; he noticed that a Sadhu was carelessly lying in the centre of his garden, not bothered about the passers-by. Akbar was shocked to see this. How could a stranger in ragged clothes, rest there right in the middle of the palace garden? He got so angry that he decided to punish his guards for letting this Sadhu in the premises of the palace. Furiously he walked over to the Sadhu and prodded him with the tip of his embroidered slipper.

"Hey, you!" he cried. "Who are you and how dare you sleep here like this?"

The Sadhu opened his eyes calmly and sat up slowly. Dazed, he asked looking at the emperor straight in his eyes, "Huzoor, is this your garden?"

"Yes!" shouted Akbar. "This garden, those rose bushes, the fountain beyond that, the courtyard, the palace, this fort, this empire, everything here belongs to me!"

Slowly the Sadhu stood up and asked, "And what about the river, and the city, and this country Huzoor?"

"Yes, they all belong to me," said the emperor. "Now, if you've got the answers to your questions, you may please get out of here!"

"Ah," said the Sadhu, undisturbed by the emperor's reply. "And before you, who owned the garden and fort and city?"

"My father, of course," said the emperor. Though he was irritated, he found the conversation with the Sadhu getting interesting. Akbar always loved philosophical discussions and felt that there was something different about this man in ragged clothes.

"And who owned it before him?" the Sadhu asked quietly.

"His father, my grandfather."

"Ah," said the Sadhu. So all the belongings that you claim to be yours belongs to you only for this lifetime. Just like before you it belonged to your father and before that your grandfather; after you it will belong to your son and then your grandson, and so on. Am I right?

"Yes," said Akbar, already in deep thought.

"So our stay here is temporary, right?"

"Yes."

The Sadhu asked. "No one owns a temporary accommodation. We don't own the shade of a tree on the side of a road. We only stop and rest for a while and proceed on our journey. Some people

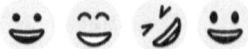

have come before us, and some will come after us. Isn't it?"

"Yes," said the emperor quietly.

"So your garden, your palace, your fort, your empire...all these are the places you will stay only for this lifetime. When you die, they will no longer belong to you. After you, all this will belong to your son."

Emperor Akbar nodded. "You see Huzoor, the whole world is like a Dharmashala - a temporary accommodation. We rest here while we are in this physical body. So how can anything here belong to anybody? We are just the passengers on this earth and have to leave one day. This is the eternal truth," Sadhu said slowly, thinking very hard.

The emperor smiled at him. He had learned his lesson.

The Sadhu, bowing down removed his beard, and the turban said in his normal voice, "Jahanpanah, please forgive me, but it was my way to make you think about life!"

The emperor immediately recognized his favourite minister and said, "Birbal, You are wiser than most of the philosophers I have met. Come, let's sit and discuss more on this."

How very profound! What is it on this earth that belongs to us?

As Bhagwat Geeta says, "What did you lose that you cry about? What did you bring with you, which you think you have lost? What did you produce, which you think got destroyed? You did not bring anything - whatever you have, you received from here. Whatever you have given, you have given only here. Whatever you took, you took from God. Whatever you gave, you gave to him. You came empty-handed; you will leave empty-handed. What is yours today, belonged to someone else yesterday, and will belong to someone else the day after tomorrow. You are mistakenly enjoying the thought that this is yours. It is this false happiness that is the cause of your sorrows."

Most of the sufferings are a result of the need to possess and the attachment to those possessions. My house, my money, my car, my children, my husband, my friends and so on. What needs to be understood is that all these things are transient. Even we are not permanent residents on this planet Earth. We have come here to enact a specific role, and we have to exit when that role is over. The character could be that of a prince or popper, or that of a man or a woman. At times, there could be more challenging roles than those that come our way. Our responsibility is to give our best performance. This is the simple truth of life that we forget and live as if we own everything, right from things to people. We take the onus of everything on us. This is what that makes us unhappy in life. But if we can understand the real purpose of coming on this earth and follow it, we can live every moment happily.

"Life is like a piano: the white keys represent happiness, the black keys show sadness. But as you go through life's journey, remember that the black keys make music too..." - Unknown.

The universal laws govern life, and the process of life is unfolding in front of us.

Each one of us has to go through our share of success and failure,

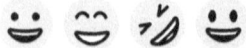

in every area of our life be it relationships, career, health or wealth. No human being born on this planet could ever escape this phenomenon - be it the Buddha or the president of the United States. Once we can understand, that this is what life is all about, then even failure cannot bring us unhappiness. We need to trust the universal process. If we believe that everything that happens in our life is for our highest good, if we can adopt this thought, nothing can stop us from being happy and peaceful.

There is a beautiful prayer, "God, grant me the serenity to accept the things I cannot change; the courage to change the things I can; and the wisdom to know the difference." Certain things happen in our life that are beyond our control, but we lose our peace and happiness over them. Such things include other people's behaviour, worries about our future, some situations and challenges in life and so on. Adopting the mantra that 'whatever happens is for our highest good' gives a lot of respite as that unburdens us from the responsibility of a doer and acceptance comes easily.

If we can adopt this attitude, life will be a beautiful journey filled with happiness.

Reflections:
Once you develop a higher understanding of life, you look at everything that happens with a heightened consciousness, and acceptance and letting go comes quickly.

Step to Happiness:
Believe that everything
that happens in your life
happens for the highest
good.

Happiness Mantra:
Just for today, I
accept life happily,
as it unfolds in front
of me.

THE 21-DAY HAPPINESS CHALLENGE

Since you are on this page, I assume that you have completed reading the book. I invite you to take the 21-days happiness challenge. There is one suggestion for each day, and likewise, there are 21 suggestions. If you follow them diligently, I can assure you that by the end of the 21st day you will be a happier person on this planet irrespective of your situations or circumstances. The condition is that the practice of each day should be carried forward every day with a new suggestion. Are you ready to take up the HAPPINESS CHALLENGE...?

Day 1: CHOICE

Acknowledge that you are blessed with the power to choose.

You can choose to let the situations affect you or not affect you.

You can choose to learn from your mistakes or brood over them.

You can choose to be confident or afraid.

You can choose to be sad or happy.

You can choose......exercise that choice. Today, consciously make the best possible choices that will take your life in the direction you want it to go. For example, if somebody shouts at you, choose

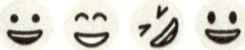

whether you want to get affected by it or not.

Day 2: EMPATHY

Try being an empathetic person. Today, take 10 minutes of your time to think if you have had any misunderstandings with anyone around you in the recent past, that may have strained the relationship. Connect with that person and try to understand his/her perspective that led to the misunderstanding, in an unbiased way.

Day 3: ATTITUDE

Try to build up a positive attitude. The world is how we perceive it to be. Be conscious and change your perspective of looking at everything today in a positive way.

Day 4: COURAGE

Today, attempt at least one thing that you are afraid of. It could be something that you are apprehensive about, it could be one of your unfounded fears, or it could be something that you have told yourself that you cannot do. For example, it could be talking to an unknown person, or public speaking, or driving on a steep slope, or trekking or anything that makes out step out of your comfort zone.

Day 5: COMPARISON

Unknowingly we tend to compare ourselves with people around us. Today, be aware of your thoughts and do not compare yourself with anyone. You are unique and respect your uniqueness. Acknowledge and appreciate yourself for what you are.

Day 6: PASSION

Passion has the power to enrich your life and make it meaningful and happy. If you are already passionate about something take some time out and do it. If you haven't found your passion yet, then today is the time to discover your passion. Or, just do what you love at least for some time during the day. It could be reading, writing, singing, dancing, painting, running, cooking or whatever that makes you forget everything else in the world.

Day 7: RELATIONSHIP

Call your friend, family, relative, or acquaintance without any agenda. Just tell them what you feel about them, how important they are in your life and how much you value the relationship. Meet up with someone you haven't met for a very long time. Just have a soulful conversation with them over coffee, lunch or dinner without your cell phones.

Day 8: PRESENT MOMENT

Today try to live every moment consciously. Be present in the now. For today, don't think either about your past or your future. If your thoughts drift from the present moment, bring them back to the now. Meditate for thirty minutes, and observe your breath and be conscious of your breath.

Day 9: DREAMS

Think about all the dreams you had as a child, and faded away as you

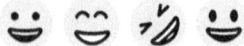

grew older. Make a list and do at least one thing out of those today.

Day 10: WORRY

Realize that worry is a futile emotion. Today, consciously decide that you will not worry about anything. Embrace the day as it unfolds and go with the flow.

Day 11: EGO

Step out of your ego self and act. Be humble in your behaviour towards others.

Day 12: NON JUDGEMENTAL

Do not judge anybody. Every person is right in his or her own space. Acknowledge that. No one is perfect, not even you. Embrace the imperfection of yourself and others.

Day 13: KINDNESS

Practice the act of kindness. Go out and help people who are not as fortunate as you are. It could be as simple as helping an old person cross the road.

Day 14: ANGER

Be aware of this emotion. If you feel your anger rising, or you feel irritable, focus on your breath. You will slowly return to the peaceful state. The key is awareness and being conscious about your breathing.

Day 15: BEING YOU

For the entire day today, repeat the affirmation, "I acknowledge and appreciate my uniqueness and accept and love myself the way I am."

Day 16: MIRACLES

Look at the world today with the eyes of wonderment. Don't take anything for granted and you will see how beautiful the world is.

Day 17: DETACHMENT

Do you value your material possessions more than people around you? Do you fret and mull over, if your maid breaks something in the house or your son spills juice on your sofa or your mobile falls, and the screen breaks? And does it take you a long time to accept that situation? Invest today in contemplating on these questions. If the answer is 'yes,' means you are too attached to the material things. Do self-talk and tell yourself that it's not a big deal. It is only an object, and you can't waste your energy and time over that.

Day 18: PEACE

If you look outside of you, you will always find chaos, and if you look within, you will find peace. It is generally our thoughts that disturb our peace. Today, focus within by focusing on your breath. If you focus on your breath for a longer time, your thoughts will disappear, and you will experience peace.

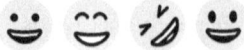

Day 19: GRATITUDE

Be grateful for everything in your life – good or bad. Good and bad is only a perspective. Sometimes the things that we perceive as bad lead to something good in the future. Be grateful for every small thing in your life and make a gratitude list. You can also thank people who have added value to your life; however, you have never expressed your gratitude towards them. Call them and say 'Thank you' or you can even do it mentally.

Day 20: CONTENTMENT

Be content for what you have today. Even if it is not the best or what you want it to be; think that it could have been worse. Contentment brings peace and happiness.

Day 21: UNDERSTANDING

Believe that everything that happens in your life is for your highest good. With our limited perspective, we cannot see the whole picture and hence get disheartened. But once you understand this simple truth you can be happy every moment.

Once you complete this happiness challenge, urge your friends and family to take it up. Happiness is contagious.

Mahatma Gandhi said, "Be the change you wish to see in the world." So let us all do our bit. Let us all contribute to making this planet a HAPPY ABODE, by being happy ourselves and spreading it around.

Cheers!

DAILY REMINDERS

1. Choose wisely

2. Empathise with others

3. Develop a positive attitude

4. Act courageously

5. Never compare

6. Live Passionately

7. Value your relationships

8. Live in the moment

9. Follow your dreams

10. Stop worrying

11. Don't act out of ego

12. Be non-judgemental

13. Be Kind

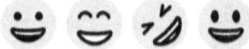

14. Let go of anger

15. Be yourself

16. Believe in miracles

17. Practice detachment

18. Be peaceful

19. Be grateful

20. Be content

21. Be aware